CW01304391

Haunted Healthcare 2

Also by Richard Estep

In Search of the Paranormal

Haunted Longmont

The World's Most Haunted Hospitals

Trail of Terror

Colorado UFOs

The Devil's Coming to Get Me

The Fairfield Haunting

The Farnsworth House Haunting

The Dead Below

The Horrors of Fox Hollow Farm

As co-author

The Haunting of Asylum 49

Spirits of the Cage

A Haunting at Farrar

Haunted Healthcare 2

Medical Professionals and Patients Share
Their Encounters with the Paranormal

Richard Estep

Copyright 2019 Richard Estep

All rights reserved

For the cast, crew, and creators of *Haunted Hospitals* and *Paranormal 911*.

It is a pleasure and a privilege to work with you all.

Contents

Foreword by MJ Dickson	*1*
Introduction	*13*
Chapter 1 – Help Me	*17*
Chapter 2 – He Made it to Heaven	*33*
Chapter 3 – The Army Man	*41*
Chapter 4 – Code Blue	*55*
Chapter 5 – The Hanging	*63*
Chapter 6 – The Offices of Death	*75*
Chapter 7 – The Matron's Dog	*83*
Chapter 8 – A Long Night	*91*
Chapter 9 – Bed, Bath, and Beyond	*99*
Chapter 10 – Remembering Nathan	*115*
Chapter 11 – Wolf Man	*125*
Chapter 12 – Dead Man Walking	*139*
Chapter 13 – Dark Passenger	*149*
Chapter 14 – The Boy	*159*
Chapter 15 – Asylum	*169*
Acknowledgments 209	

Foreword

There are many things about this life that we don't understand, and there's even more about the afterlife that is a mystery to us. For more than a decade, I've worked as a paranormal investigator. I've traveled around the world seeking answers to life's deepest mysteries, hoping to capture enough evidence of the paranormal to gain a better understanding of it myself.

What happens when we die? Why do some of us remain here on this earthly plane, while others move on? Why are some spirits stuck in a 'Purgatory' of sorts? Why is it that it seems to be hospitals and asylums which hold some of the saddest hauntings and residual energy?

Hospitals are a place of death *and* new life, and therefore, there is just as much joy, love, and happiness as there is grief, sadness, or anger. Hospitals, by their very nature, are pretty scary places to be, at least for the majority of us. The pungent smell of disinfectant floats through the air down the labyrinth of corridors, bright lights illuminating the sterile rooms which all seem so unwelcoming, as the moans of patients in pain reverberate through the building and nurses scurry around between them.

The constant, annoying beep of machinery adds to the already-unnerving atmosphere. Needless to say, I am not a fan. The less time I can spend in a hospital for any reason, the better.

Unfortunately for me, this was not the case in 2015. I was admitted for a long and quite unpleasant stay in a Birmingham city hospital — an extremely *haunted* hospital — in the heart of the U.K.

After suffering severe back pain and getting an MRI scan, I was rushed to the hospital for a life-saving surgery. It was a bitterly cold and foggy November morning. As I was taken through the ward for pre-surgery prep, the surgeon explained the procedure to me, but all I could hear was my heartbeat pounding in my ears, drowning out the surgeon's voice.

My head was reeling, and the taste of blood filled my mouth. I realized I was clenching my jaw, fighting back the tears. The thin hospital gown was not exactly keeping me warm on that winter morning, and yet I could feel the sweat forming on my brow, my nerves making me feel sick to my stomach. I had just been diagnosed with a large tumor, and rushed in for surgery, so to say that I was an emotional wreck was an understatement.

I lay back on the bed, closed my eyes, and took as few deep breaths before they wheeled me into the next room, where I was greeted by the anesthetist, whose youthful looks made me doubt that he had much in the way of experience.

I felt the panic well up in my chest, and my stomach tightened into a knot. As he held my forearm, the doctor read the tattoo of my father's military tags. To my surprise, he knew the regiment, and mentioned that he had worked as a medic in the army; he had served in the same countries as my father.

Knowing that he was a military man himself, instantly put me at ease, and brought me a lot of comfort during an extremely stressful time. As he asked me to count backward from ten, I felt the sensation of liquid flowing into my vein as the anesthetic was administered.

I don't remember getting past number seven.

The surgery took over three hours, and thankfully, it was a great success. I woke up in the recovery ward, in great pain and still very groggy. The nurse welcomed me back, checking my blood pressure and giving me some pills to swallow down with a mouthful of cool water. After passing out for a couple more hours, I woke up in my private room, confused and disoriented. At least I wasn't in as much pain.

As I looked around the room, trying to focus, I heard the surgeon telling my husband that the surgery had gone well. Relief washed over me, and I burst into tears. I was so happy to see my husband standing at my bedside. Later, when visiting hours were over, he kissed me goodbye and told me to get some rest. I fell straight into a deep sleep.

I woke up at around three o'clock in the morning and switched on the light. As I lay there, looking around the room, a short, elderly lady in her seventies walked into the room. She was wearing a floral nightdress, and sat down at the end of my bed. I was completely bewildered! She offered me a warm, welcoming smile, while I tried to make sense of who she was and what she was doing there. I pushed myself up on the bed, never breaking eye contact, but when I began asking her what she was doing in my room, she disappeared.

She was just *gone*, vanished into thin air.

Shaking my head, I stared at the empty chair in utter disbelief. I tried to rationalize what I had just experienced. Perhaps it was due to the pain medication. Perhaps I was dreaming. There was absolutely no way that had just happened…right?

I hit the button to call the nurse. My heart was racing, the adrenaline pumping. The nurse came into the room and asked if I was okay, adding that I looked like I had just seen a ghost. While she wrapped the blood pressure cuff around my arm, I blurted out the question: "Has anyone experienced anything *weird* in this room?"

She smiled, and told me that several patients had reported seeing a lady in her seventies, wearing a floral night dress. The nurse went on to tell me that, according to these eyewitnesses, the lady had walked into the room and sat in the same chair at the end of the bed, smiled at them, and then disappeared...

...the exact same thing I had just experienced.

I couldn't sleep after that. I lay in bed, staring at the ceiling, thinking about the fact that I was in a haunted room, and wondering who this lady was and why she was there. I replayed the event over and over in my head — such a brief moment in time, that had had such a huge impact on me. It got me thinking about just how haunted hospitals really are, how many other people had paranormal experiences and brushed them off, thinking that it was due to nothing more than their medication.

One thing that struck me was that, in the few seconds that I was looking at her, not once did I feel threatened or that I was in harm's way. She seemed sweet, gentle, and very, very real.

The reason I am telling you the entire story of my surgery is to point out the fact that, within one day, I experienced so many different emotions, ranging from anxiety and fear prior to my surgery, to happiness, relief, and love when I saw my husband — and then, later, the confusion and shock.

I was just one person within those hospital walls. Just imagine how many people are experiencing those and other emotions inside a hospital on any given day. From intense sadness surrounding the last, dying breath of a loved one, to the joy of a new mother who has just held her baby for the first time, these strong emotions must play some role in the hauntings.

Perhaps spirits are able to feed on these emotions; this energy could be the main reason why we experience more hauntings in hospitals. Could it be that the majority of the hauntings are purely residual energy, trapped in the building from these intense moments? Whatever the case may be, I realized very quickly that this was going to be a very long stay.

Fast-forward to March, 2016.

I received a voice mail message from my doctor, asking

me to see her as soon as possible. This time, I would be going to a different Birmingham hospital. Worry set in, and I immediately made an appointment for the following morning.

The next day, I arrived at the appointed time and took a deep breath as my husband, Duncan, lovingly squeezed my hand to reassure me. We met with my doctor, who told me that this would be my pre-surgical admission. Confused, Duncan and I looked at one another, while the doctor explained that, due to the type of tumor that had been removed during my first surgery, they thought it would be best for me to have a full hysterectomy.

I had been told during my teens that, due to a motorcycle accident I had had when I was fifteen, I would never be able to have children, so this didn't come as too great a shock. She instructed my husband to go home and pack me a bag, while they admitted me for surgery that would take place the following day.

Everything happened really fast, and before I knew it, I was out of surgery and waking up in the recovery ward. This time around, I felt a lot more at ease, already knowing what to expect from the surgical procedure. The team were simply wonderful!

I opened my eyes and lay there for a while, just looking around, when I noticed a nurse sitting down at a nearby table, filling out my paperwork. Weakly, I raised a hand in the air and proclaimed: "This one has risen!" That got her attention, and made her giggle. She came over to check my blood pressure and assess my pain level.

The nurse informed me that I would not immediately be moved into a private room, and that they wanted to keep an eye on me; I was therefore moved onto the main ward, which also happened to be the oldest part of the hospital.

I woke up a few hours later with another nurse checking my blood pressure. As I looked up and past her, I could see my father sitting on the side of my bed. This was very reassuring. My father had passed away in December 2011, but I was seeing him so vividly, feeling his energy and emotion so strongly, that all I could do was smile. I could even feel the indentation on the mattress next to me.

My father never said a word, but I knew that I was going to be just fine. Little did I know that the worst news was still to come.

I remember looking up at the nurse and telling her that my dad was sitting on the bed next to me. The nurse's head shot up, her eyes widening with shock as she looked from me to the bed and back again. I put my head back, closed my eyes, and let the anesthetic take me away once more. It was only when I woke up later that night that I realized I had almost given the poor nurse a heart attack, by telling her that I could see my father sitting on the edge of my bed. She had no idea that I am a psychic medium. The poor woman must have thought I was about to kick the bucket, as I was seeing people from the other side!

After three days in hospital, I was able to get up and walk around a little. I had refused any strong painkillers, settling instead for paracetamol and ibuprofen as I hate having a fuzzy head; I rely on my Spidey-senses a lot, and pain meds tend to dull them.

This hospital was super active; I picked up on *so many* different spirits. Yet again, this experience got me thinking, if my father was there for me, then it was highly likely that each patient had a family member or two with them, along with the spirits who just hang around the hospital. One thing was for sure, it was a tremendously busy place!

Around mid-day, they moved me into my own private room, which was just a couple of metres away from the nurses' station. I am generally a night owl, so at around four o'clock in the morning, I got out of bed and walked to the station. Three nurses were sitting at the counter, doing their paperwork by the light of a single lamp.

Even though the lights were dimmed, I could see that all of the other patients on the ward were asleep in their beds. I asked if I could please have a cup of coffee, and the nurses invited me to sit with them for a bit while I drank it. They pulled up a chair for me, and we chatted away.

About twenty minutes had gone by, when I suddenly saw movement out of the corner of my eye. A shadow had walked across the ward and into my room.

I leaned back in my chair, to see whether there were any other entrances to the ward. One of the nurses asked me if I was okay. I told her that I had just seen what looked a lot like the shadow of a tall man, walking across the ward and going into my private room.

The nurses exchanged a despairing look. Reluctantly, one of them grabbed a flashlight and told the other two to accompany her as they went to investigate my room. I followed closely behind them. The opportunity to investigate something paranormal in the oldest ward of the oldest Birmingham city hospital was a chance I was not passing up — and besides, it was *my* room!

As we entered the room and switched on the light, we

felt a gust of cold wind move past us into the doorway. I shuddered, and the hair on the back of my neck stood on end. Although there was nothing out of place in my room, the atmosphere felt heavy.

Going back to the nurses' station, we settled back into our seats. The nurses began to tell me about the strange things they had each experienced on the ward. This was not the first time this shadowy figure had been seen, and I am certain that it will not be the last.

I had spoken to Richard Estep online, and finally met him in person in November 2018 at my paranormal convention, the Sage Paracon, where he was one of my guest speakers. I was honored when he invited me along on a research investigation, and asked me to write the foreword of this book…no pressure, right?

Richard is a fantastic author; in fact, he is one of my personal favorites, so I have no doubt that you will enjoy reading the stories within these pages. I am currently working an ongoing private case, which involves a gentleman who is experiencing a severe 'haunting' — however, I am not entirely convinced that what he is experiencing is paranormal. I believe it to be a case of extreme delusion, manifesting as something 'supernatural.'

In his mind, he is being haunted. There is a whole different side to how medical conditions play a massive role in what people believe to be a haunting.

From ghostly apparitions walking through wards, to the stories of people seeing their loved ones appear near them shortly before passing away, there is no shortage of stories when it comes to working in hospitals and mental health facilities.

Just ask any healthcare professional.

— MJ Dickson

.

Introduction

So…why write a second volume of *Haunted Healthcare?* I wrote the first book for one very simple reason. Over the course of the seventeen years that I have spent working as an Emergency Medical Technician (EMT) first, and then later as a paramedic, I have never gone to great lengths to conceal my interest in all things paranormal. It didn't take long for me to develop a reputation as being 'that ghost guy,' and soon afterward, some of the medical professionals I encountered began coming to me with their own ghostly experiences.

In between the release of *Haunted Healthcare* and this second volume, I filmed the second season of the TV series *Haunted Hospitals*, and season one of *Paranormal 911*, which expanded its scope to cover the ghostly encounters experienced by police officers, firefighters, and EMS providers during the course of their duties.

As both shows began to take off, airing on the Travel Channel in the United States and various other TV stations around the world, I began to get more and more emails from medical professionals who wanted to share their own stories of brushes with the paranormal.

These stories ran the gamut from disturbing and chilling, to the heartwarming and empowering. Take, for example, the following experience, submitted by reader Judy Leesee. Back in 2016, she and her husband visited a mutual friend, John, in a major Baltimore hospital.

As they entered the room, the sound of growling suddenly came from one of the corners. Judy looked carefully but could see no cause for it whatsoever.

The two visitors took seats next to John's bed, directly beneath the window. His wife was also present at his bedside. Then came the growling again, louder this time. It sounded like a dog, which was patently ridiculous: no dogs were allowed in the hospital rooms.

"Does anybody hear that growling?" Judy finally asked. All three of the other people in the room shook their heads to indicate that they did not.

Then, John and his wife looked at one another. "That must be Malachai," John said, referring to his pet dog. He looked over at Judy's husband, Jay, and chuckled. "Malachai died a few months back. He never did like Jay much. Whenever he'd come over to the house, that dog would growl at him and bare his teeth. I'd have to hold him back…"

Many skeptics would dismiss such stories as being little more than the product of an overly-active imagination, a charge that they like to level at the vast majority of paranormal reports. Yet it must be pointed out that the sheer volume of eyewitness testimony, coming as it does from doctors, nurses, technicians, paramedics, patients, and family members, speaks for itself. As the old saying goes, quantity has a quality all of its own.

Some of the accounts I was told fit the classic mold of the death-bed experience, whereas others were nothing short of outright bizarre. All of them were fascinating, and I spoke with many of those who contacted me in person, helping them look for a non-paranormal explanation.

In some cases, we found one; in many, we did not.

Based upon the positive reviews, readers seemed to enjoy the first volume of *Haunted Healthcare*, and therefore, writing a second seemed to be a no-brainer. The story which resonated the most with people was that of my friend Kyle, who has spent many years bravely battling terminal cancer. Kyle was deeply moved by the overwhelmingly positive response to his story, and found it very comforting to hear that his story had been an inspiration for so many people. He and I still hang out on a regular basis. His cancer continues to advance, and he is fully prepared for the fact that his life is now coming to an end. His encounters with the spirits of his departed friends are still going on, and I continue to be awed and humbled by his phenomenal courage. Being given the honor of sharing his story with the world was, without a doubt, the best thing about writing the first book in the *Haunted Healthcare* series.

And now, on to the second. These pages are full of accounts of apparitions of the dead, phantom footsteps, disembodied voices, and even shapeshifters(!). I hope you enjoy reading them as much as I enjoyed gathering the experiences and interviewing the witnesses.

If you work in the field of healthcare or the emergency medical services, and would like to share a paranormal experience with the readers of *Haunted Healthcare*, please send me an email at richard@richardestep.net.

Onward, through the fog!

Richard Estep
Longmont, Colorado
June 2019

CHAPTER ONE
Help Me

Ambulance standbys tend to share one thing in common with paranormal investigations: most of the time, they both involve sitting around with a whole lot of nothing going on.

But there are exceptions.

The hospital, a major facility located in the big city, was undergoing some major reconstruction work. Sometimes things can go wrong when construction workers start knocking holes in walls, and so Trish, a paramedic, and her partner Jeff (not his real name) were assigned to stand by with their EMS unit, just in case there was a problem that required one of the patients to transported to a different hospital.

Jeff was a 'baby paramedic' — in other words, he was newly-certified and hadn't been out of paramedic school for very long. Trish had worked with him before, however, and had found him to be a level-headed kind of guy that was cool under pressure. She enjoyed picking up shifts with him.

Both paramedics were expecting a quiet night. Each of them had worked on countless standbys where the most exciting thing that happened was scrolling through their

Facebook feed or deciding where to go to pick up lunch.

They were sitting in the ambulance cab, chatting about nothing in particular, when the radio squawked.

"Dispatch to Medic Twelve."

Trish picked up the mic and pushed the talk button. "Go for Medic Twelve."

"Medic Twelve, I need you to head over to the main emergency department entrance. We've got one coming out of there for you."

"They're not doing any construction in the E.D." Jeff was puzzled. "Wonder where we're taking the patient?"

"Show Medic Twelve en-route." Trish shrugged and hung up the mic. She put the ambulance into gear. "Guess we'll find out when we get there…"

The emergency department was right around the corner. When the EMS crew arrived, they were met by one of the nurses, who was standing in the ambulance bay. Trish and Jeff hopped out and began to pull on their nitrile examination gloves.

"Hi there. I'm Trish, and this is my partner, Jeff. What do we have?" Trish was polite, but all business. The nurse introduced herself in return. She immediately began to get an odd feeling about the nurse's demeanor. The nurse seemed, for want of a better word, embarrassed.

After working for years in emergency medicine, Trish was experienced in the art of reading people. She was more than capable of recognizing the signs that something wasn't quite right. It didn't have to be a major red flag; sometimes, it was just a subtle little cue that told her something was off.

The nurse shifted uncomfortably, pausing for an awkward moment before explaining.

"Uh, well, we don't actually have a patient for you, as such..." she began.

"No patient?" Jeff asked, not understanding. "Then why are we here?"

"If you wouldn't mind getting your bed, I'll explain as we go." The bed, also known as the *pram, cot,* or *gurney,* depending on which part of the country you were working in, was a bright yellow wheeled stretcher. Trish and Jeff slid it out of the back of the ambulance, keeping one ear on the nurse as she began to tell them a somewhat macabre story.

"The power to the basement has been out for most of the day," the nurse said, keeping pace with the medics as they rolled their bed around to the far side of the hospital. "All of the coolers are out down there."

"Coolers..." A metaphorical light bulb went on over

Trish's head. "Hey, the *morgue* is down there."

"That's right." Now the source of her embarrassment became clear. "We shipped out most of the bodies, but, well...we forgot one."

There was an awkward silence, broken only by the squeaking of one of the wheels on the bed. Finally, Trish said, "You...*forgot*...*one?*"

*You **forget** your car keys,* Trish was thinking. *You don't forget a **corpse**.*

"Hey, accidents happen," the nurse said, downplaying the fact that the hospital staff had managed to let the presence of somebody's loved one being in the morgue slip their mind. "Anyway, I spoke to the funeral home. They're not able to take him tonight. Their earliest availability is tomorrow afternoon."

"Won't he be starting to smell a little by then?" Jeff asked, meaning no disrespect. Once the power had gone out, the air in the morgue would have begun trending upward toward normal room temperature. That, in turn, would have accelerated the decomposition process. It wouldn't be too long before the lone body started to get a little ripe.

"Absolutely," she agreed, "and that's why you're here. I called over to [a neighboring hospital] and they've kindly agreed to take John Doe for us, and store him in their morgue until the funeral director can come and pick him up."

"And we're his ride over there," Trish said, filling in the blanks.

"Right." The nurse went down a short ramp and badged them through a set of double security doors. "You guys know the way to the morgue?"

They didn't, but the security guard that came to join them did. He led the EMS crew through the doors and into a dark hallway, one that stretched out in front of them until it disappeared into complete blackness. Jeff steered the bed from the front while Trish pushed it along from the back, trying to keep up with the guard's long stride.

This isn't going to be so bad, Trish thought. *The other hospital's only a few blocks away. We'll be done in thirty minutes. An hour, tops.*

The further they got into the depths of the hospital, the darker it became. Windows are rarely a consideration when they construct hospital basements, and it now became apparent that this was one of the parts of the building to which the power had been cut.

Incredibly, the security guard didn't have a flashlight. Thinking ahead, Trish and Jeff had brought along the two small pocket flashlights that were carried on each emergency ambulance. Unfortunately, when they pulled the flashlights out and tried to switch them on, they found that the batteries were completely drained.

"Figures," Trish grumbled, clicking the on/off switch a few times. It was impossible to tell whether the flashlight batteries had been dead from the moment they had first picked them up, or if something in the hospital could have caused it to happen.

When she finally looked back on this call afterward, with the benefit of hindsight, Trish would come to believe in the latter of the two explanations.

"I should have taken it as the first sign that this was going to be a truly messed-up transport," she laughs.

Reaching into her back pocket, Trish pulled out her cell phone. Giving thanks for the fact that it had a built-in light of its own, she powered it up and used it to illuminate the way for Jeff.

Ambulances and dead bodies generally don't go together. If a patient were to pass away in the back of an ambulance and be pronounced dead there, the vehicle would normally become a scene that the coroner would be required to investigate, in order to ensure that the death was a natural one. This would usually entail a wait of several hours (coroners and their assistants are busy people) and all that time, the ambulance is out of service, a valuable resource that can no longer be sent on 911 calls and patient transports.

What this means in practice is that most patients are either pronounced dead at the scene, with the body being touched and moved as little as possible, or resuscitated until their arrival at the hospital, in the hopes that the receiving Emergency Department physician will be able to use their skills to successfully revive them...and if not, then the patient will be pronounced dead in the hospital, and subsequently sent to the morgue.

On some rare occasions, however, ambulances *do* transport dead bodies. This is usually done as a courtesy to the coroner or to the sending hospital, when the deceased has already been determined to have died under normal circumstances. In such cases, the ambulance is essentially acting as a hearse.

A loud clatter made Trish jump halfway out her skin. She had bumped into a table with her hip, rattling some medical equipment. She laughed, as much to try and diffuse the tension as anything else. This place was making her uneasy. As she and Jeff got closer to the morgue, the acerbic smell of disinfectant in the air grew stronger. She figured that it wasn't a coincidence.

It was starting to feel just a little too much like a horror movie.

The squeak of the security guard's boots on the floor suddenly stopped. From somewhere up ahead, Trish could hear the sound of a door being opened.

"Morgue's in here," the guard said, leading Jeff in through the open doorway. Trish pushed the gurney inside, being careful not to hit the doorframe. The thing handled like a shopping cart with a busted wheel.

The morgue was silent and still.

Suddenly, an ice-cold sensation rippled down Trish's back. She shivered at the unmistakable feeling of 'somebody walking over her grave,' as some people liked to call it.

Though she couldn't quite say why, Trish's hackles were going up. She tried to shrug it off. After all, she was standing inside the *morgue* for heaven's sake, in almost total darkness. It was perfectly understandable that the hairs on the back of her neck would be standing on end.

Then came the voice.

"Help." It whispered into her right ear. Seconds later, it added, "Me."

Help me.

She jumped.

The voice had sounded like that of an old man, with a distinctly raspy, out-of-breath quality to it. As a paramedic, she knew what it sounded like when somebody was struggling to breathe, unable to move air, and that was exactly what the man's voice had sounded like to her.

Trish spun around, looking over her right shoulder. The only shapes she could make out in the darkness were those of Jeff and the security guard. Neither of them was responsible, so who else could have spoken?

There was also the fact that both Jeff and the security guard were younger men, whereas the voice had been that of a much older man. Neither of them had reacted, or given any indication that they had heard the voice themselves.

Perhaps she had imagined the whole thing, Trish reasoned, trying to a get a grip on herself and slow down her racing heart rate. It was just a dark room that smelled of antiseptic, after all — a room that was usually filled with dead bodies, but now contained only the one.

"Hey!" Jeff yelled, his voice high-pitched and startled. He scuttled away to his left, as though recoiling from something that Trish couldn't see. The security guard was looking in all directions, searching for some kind of threat.

"What is it?" Trish demanded.

"Something just grabbed my right *f****** LEG!*" Jeff might have been a newer paramedic, but he had been an experienced EMT for several years before that. He was not normally given to panic or becoming overly excited.

Now, that had all gone out the window. He sounded truly frightened, and from the sound of his voice, Trish suspected that he was on the verge of seriously freaking out.

"Dude, relax," she said, Trish's own unnerving experience temporarily forgotten in her desire to calm her partner down. "It was probably just another table or something like that. You bumped into it in the dark, like I almost did outside in the hallway."

In an attempt to allay his fears, she swept her phone's light around in a circle, illuminating the floor and walls. The tile floor was completely bare, except for the stainless steel table on which bodies were laid for examination, which was on the opposite side of the room. There was nothing that Jeff's leg could have come into contact with.

Based on the rate of his breathing, Trish suspected that he was beginning to hyperventilate. *That* definitely wasn't a good thing.

Now satisfied that there was no physical threat, the security guard was also trying his best to calm Jeff down. He needed to slow down his breathing and relax a little. Trish was on edge herself by now, being more than a little spooked by her surroundings, and Jeff's freakout wasn't helping any.

It was then that she felt a cold, bony hand run down the length of her bare right arm. Trish jerked her hand away. It had felt for all the world as if somebody had been trying to grab her hand and wrist.

"Damn!" she hissed, recoiling as if she had been stung.

"What?" Jeff demanded, his voice full of apprehension.

"Nothing. Let's just get this thing done, shall we?"

The security guard was in total agreement with them. He opened up the door that led to the refrigerated room in which the bodies were stored.

A wall of cold air wafted out of what was basically an enormous freezer, the entire contents of which were a single black body bag. Working in dim, near-dark conditions, Trish and Jeff squatted down on their haunches and took hold of the carrying handles. On the count of three they both stood up, lifting the body along with them, and swung it gently over onto their cot. Both paramedics went about their task as respectfully as possible. It did not sit well with them that this poor man, who they would come to find out was a veteran, had basically been forgotten by the hospital authorities, and they were determined to make his transfer to the next hospital as dignified as they could possibly manage.

To that end, they straightened the body bad on top of their bed and then strapped it down with three sets of seat belts. Once they were all buckled securely into place, Trish and Jeff unfolded a crisp white bed-sheet and draped it reverently over the body bag. There was a school of thought which held that, if the paramedic crew should inadvertently happen upon some patients or family members while they were wheeling their gurney out of the hospital, it might be less traumatizing for them to see a white sheet covering the body bag, rather than the bag itself. (Personally, I think it's just as likely the sheet itself is more disturbing than the featureless black bag, but that's just me…)

Fortunately, this theory was never put to the test. Trish and Jeff never ran into anybody on their return journey. They loaded the gurney up into the ambulance and secured it, then waved goodbye to a security guard who seemed only too happy to see them go. When a living patient is on board an ambulance, one of the attendants has to ride in the back with them. In this case, there was no reason for either of them to be back there, but Trish chose to stay back there anyway. She figured that the old man had spent enough time alone over the past few days. Keeping him company for just a little while longer seemed like the respectful thing to do.

It was only a few blocks to the receiving hospital. They rode in silence. Trish and Jeff were both lost in their own thoughts. For her part, Trish's mind kept going back to the hand she had felt running its way down her arm. She kept her eyes on the body bag lying on the gurney in front of her, still covered by the crisp white sheet. Her partner was a good driver, but every time the ambulance hit a pothole or divot in the road, the sheet would twitch ever so slightly, giving the illusion that the body beneath it was somehow moving.

That, she knew, was just a product of her imagination. The hand on her arm, however, had not been.

"Were you trying to tell me something?" she whispered under her breath. There was no reply.

They reached the hospital without incident. Trish had never been so glad to see the end of a transport in all her life. Jeff helped her unload the gurney from the back of the ambulance, and the two of them wheeled it through the Emergency Department doors, then took the elevator down to the basement. It was a nice change to make the journey through brightly-lit hallways this time.

Before signing the documentation to accept responsibility for the body, the staff working in the morgue that night made sure that the decedent's toe tag matched that on his medical records. Unable to help herself, Trish leaned in to take a look at the man's death certificate. The cause of death was listed as a COPD exacerbation.

COPD (Chronic Obstructive Pulmonary Disease) is a respiratory ailment that is mostly — though not exclusively — suffered by smokers, and those who have lived and worked in environments with poor air quality. COPDers, as medical professionals often refer to them, find it difficult if not impossible to catch their breath, and some of the more major exacerbations can be life-threatening. Could that have explained the quality of the voice she had heard in her ear, Trish wondered.

Help me..

She had thought at the time that it had sounded like an old man who was struggling to catch his breath. Now, she put two and two together. An old man who had died from a particularly aggressive attack of respiratory distress…

…surely that was no coincidence?

Trish and Jeff still talk about the experience to this day. Paramedics see some truly upsetting things while going about the course of their duties, and few things are sadder than a senior citizen who dies while all alone. Far too many members of the older generation are left abandoned and forgotten, not only in the United States but also throughout much of the industrialized world. This is doubly tragic when we consider the fact that these are the men and women who built our society, who have made it what it is today. Those who are veterans have also fought, killed, and been wounded in its service.

They deserve to be treated better. For just a brief few minutes, on what would prove to be his last ride before being taken to the mortuary, Trish was able to show respect to one such forgotten man.

Sometimes, that's all it takes.

CHAPTER TWO
He Made it to Heaven

Jill became a Certified Nursing Assistant (CNA) almost by accident. She was working in retail, and hating every second of it. After the birth of her daughter, a chance encounter with a friend at the children's playground led to her taking a job in an nursing home. After finding out just how much satisfaction can be derived from such work, she switched things up a little, taking a job working as a home healthcare provider for a Florida hospice. Working with the dying was extremely rewarding. She now has twenty years of experience under her belt.

"As CNAs, we have the time to really sit down and talk to people," she enthuses. "We get to talk to them about their impending death, what it's going to be like, and most importantly, we can help them prepare a little."

Her first encounters with the paranormal came during her childhood, growing up in Illinois. One room in her house was perpetually cold; the light switch in that room had a propensity for switching itself off and on. The house was haunted by the spirit of a child named Tony, who had died of leukemia in that house. This led to a lifelong interest in ghost stories.

She considers herself to be something of a sensitive or an empath, but not a psychic or a medium in the commonly-accepted sense of the term.

One of her first jobs in healthcare was working in an assisted living facility — not a true nursing home, but rather, the sort of place where senior citizens can live somewhat independently, with a little support.

It wasn't long before she realized that the elevators seemed to have developed a life of their own, going up and down with no apparent rhyme or reason. She mentioned it to one of the nurses, who wryly told her that the elevators had a habit of 'acting crazy' whenever one of the residents was about to die.

That seemed a little far-fetched to Jill at first, but at the same time, she found the idea intriguing, which was why she began to pay a little more attention to it. Right before an in-house death, the elevators would start bouncing from floor to floor without anybody having pushed the call button.

It should be pointed out that as human beings, we sometimes have a great propensity for seeing apparently meaningful patterns in things that aren't really there — faces in the fire, or *pareidolia,* is just one example. We all have an innate desire for the naturally-chaotic universe to have some kind of underlying sense or order, and our brains like nothing more than to make associative links in order to further that agenda.

As a paranormal investigator, the first thing I would have recommended if I had been asked to assess a case such as this, would be to have a maintenance technician run a thorough diagnostic check on the elevator in order to look for mechanical or electrical faults.

But things didn't end with the misbehaving elevators. Jill soon began to catch glimpses of what she believed were two male spirits. One wore white trousers and black shoes, while the other wore blue trousers. She spotted them in several parts of the assisted living facility, and knew full well that they did not live or belong there. They weren't residents, and they weren't there to visit somebody who was.

Perhaps most tellingly, the man in the white trousers was most often spotted on the elevator. On several occasions, Jill was walking toward it and was unable to hit the call button, usually because she was carrying things. Each time the doors opened, and for a split-second she would catch a glimpse of the black shoes, white trousers, and then…nothing. The figure would disappear right there in front of her, leaving behind nothing but an empty elevator car and a whole lot of questions.

The other male figure liked to wander around in the vicinity of the kitchen and dining room. She never did figure out who the two men were.

It was seven o'clock in the evening, and Jill was getting ready to help one of the residents to shower. He was the only male resident in the entire hallway. As she approached his room, she heard the sound of two men talking. The conversation seemed to be happening behind the closed door of the bathroom.

That's weird, Jill thought. *It's too late for there to be any visitor, and he's the only man in this part of the facility.*

She reached out to open the bathroom door — and the conversation instantly stopped. The bathroom was completely empty.

A few days later, Jill was introducing herself to a new resident. She was quite the interesting character, a former nun who liked to tell people that she was "eighty percent Cherokee."

"I don't want you to think I'm crazy," she said, with a slightly embarrassed smile. "But you *do* know that this place is full of spirits, right?"

Jill was all too aware of that, but feigned surprise anyway. After all, she didn't want her colleagues thinking that she was seeing things. "What do you mean?"

"Well," the old woman began, "there's the man with the white pants, for starters. Then there's his friend. He wears *blue* pants. They really love being here, you know, and they like riding the elevator.

There was absolutely no way that the former nun could possibly have known any of that. She was completely new to the facility, and even if other residents had seen the two apparitions, there would have been no time for them to have talked to her about the sightings.

For her part, Jill felt incredibly relieved that her own encounters had just been validated by a complete stranger, and a newcomer to the residential home at that.

"Do you know who they are?" she asked, intrigued.

"They were here a long time ago. They're both very nice. They try to help out whenever they can."

Jill's mind went back to all the times that the elevator had arrived exactly when she needed it to, and her hands were a little too full to call for it. Were the spirit entities either reading her mind, or watching her as she made her way through the lobby? If not, it would have to be quite the coincidence.

The new resident went on to describe the two spirits' favorite hallway. It was the one from which Jill had heard the sound of two male voices in conversation, just a few days before.

The two men, she went on, had been residents, and had been best friends during their physical lifetime. After passing on, they had stayed behind due to their fondness for what had been their last home in this world.

The same was true of two later residents, a married couple who moved in and lived there together. Each of them wore a medical alert pendant around their neck, something which could be pressed in order to summon help if they fell or hurt themselves somehow.

One evening toward the end of the year, Jill and a colleague helped the couple get into bed and settled them in for the night. As she was tucking in the sheets, the gentleman, whose name was Joe, began speaking about his own death. It came as something of a surprise to Jill, but she and her colleagued listened with empathy while he told them that he was not afraid, because he had lived a long and full life. Joe now felt as if he was ready to depart.

"Just do us one favor, please Joe," Jill said, straightening up. "When you get to Heaven, will you let us know that you arrived safely? Please?"

Solemnly, Joe promised to do just that.

The Christmas holidays came and went. Joe's wife was admitted to hospital, where she passed. Left to his own devices, he sadly died several days later. The couple's next of kin came to the facility in order to box up all of their personal possessions. On their way out, the family members turned in both of the medical alert pendants to the care staff. They wouldn't be needed any longer. Jill made sure that the pendants were disconnected and deactivated.

The room sat empty for two weeks.

It was 10:30 on a Saturday evening. Jill and her colleagues had just finished making their rounds, checking on each of their charges, and were now sitting at the nurses' station, catching up on a little paperwork.

Suddenly, all of their pagers went off. Jill's eyes widened as she looked at the tiny screen. It was a medical alert, which wasn't particularly odd in and of itself…but it was coming from Joe's pendant. The room number listed on the alert text was that which had, until recently, been home to Joe and his wife.

The nurses went straight there. When Jill opened the

door, she found exactly what she had expected to find: an empty, dark, and silent room. The medical alert pendants were still in storage, completely incapable of sending out a call for help.

That was Joe, she realized, *letting us know that he made it to Heaven...*

CHAPTER THREE

The Army Man

Gemma has made it her life's work to help care for those who cannot care for themselves. As such, she has spent many years working in residential care homes, looking after the elderly and infirm. It is grueling, challenging, and yet also extremely rewarding work — at least, in the sense of self-satisfaction (as with so many healthcare workers, those who care for our senior citizens are not paid even close to their actual value).

This has been her first and only vocation in life. Gemma began work at the age of sixteen. Straight out of school, she was employed at a nursing home that seemed, from outside appearances at least, to be a very ordinary sort of place.

She would soon learn differently.

As the new girl, Gemma was shown the ropes by some of the more senior carers. "Whatever you do," they each warned her at different times, "do *not* go into that room. And if you do have to go in there, for some reason, never go in there on your own…"

They were talking about a nondescript room, albeit one that never seemed to have a resident living in it. It was numbered 3C. Of course, telling a sixteen-year-old that she shouldn't do something is akin to waving a red rag at a bull. The first thing Gemma wanted to do was to accept this perceived challenge, get in there, and see what all the fuss was about.

Gemma waited until none of the other employees were around, then popped open the door to the forbidden room, and ducked inside. No sooner had she done so, than she immediately started to think that her colleagues might have had a point.

The atmosphere inside the empty room was, for lack of a better term, decidedly strange. Although she knew it for the stereotype that it was, Gemma really *did* feel the hairs on the back of her neck begin to prickle, and the bare skin of her arms broke out into gooseflesh. It was almost as if her body was reacting to something inside the room — something that it couldn't see, but could somehow sense nonetheless.

At first, she tried to rationalize it away. The other carers were telling her stories in an attempt to frighten the new girl, she thought, and what's more, their mysterious, enigmatic warning was beginning to work: just seconds after closing the door behind her, she was already starting to feel psyched out.

Grow up, she told herself, shaking her head. *There's nothing to be scared of.*

Still, Gemma did not like the feeling of unease that had crept up on her, and was glad to step out of the room, close the door firmly behind her, and get on with her job.

A few weeks later, there was an emergency admission

— a new resident that needed to be taken in, and on very short notice. The only room available was the dreaded 3C. When she saw the new resident for the first time, Gemma's heart immediately went out to her. She was a sweet old lady, one that was completely bed-bound, unable to care for herself or meet even her most basic needs without significant help. A series of strokes had left her almost totally immobile and dependent upon carers such as Gemma and her colleagues. Matters were complicated even further by the fact that she had recently suffered a broken hip, and had just been released from the hospital after receiving surgery to fix it — a dangerous proposition at her advanced age, as all surgeries can be.

The new patient spent her first day settling into her new room. Things seemed to go well at first, but on her second day, she became very agitated. Constantly pushing the call button in order to bring her carers running, the old lady demanded that they "get that man out of here!"

When the care assistants asked which man she was referring to, she jabbed a finger toward an empty corner of the room. 'That man,' or whatever else he may have been, seemed to be invisible.

Despite their reassurances that there was no man present in the room, she was adamant that he was still there. Curious, Gemma asked what the man looked like. The description that the old lady provided was very precise and detailed: the man was roughly six feet, two inches tall, about thirty years of age, and was wearing a British Army uniform — yet when he talked to her, the man spoke in a language which wasn't English.

The hairs rising on the back of her neck, Gemma looked toward the area of the room in which he had supposed to be standing. "Is he still there?"

"No," the old lady shook her head. "He's gone now."

Gemma had gotten a good handle on her new charge's mental state, and had found her to be fully alert and oriented to her environment and everything that was going on. She had been a little distressed by appearance of the invisible intruder, but seemed mollified now that he was gone, and so Gemma felt comfortable leaving her on her own for a while.

Leaving the door to room 3C ajar, Gemma told the old lady that she was going to get some work done, but would be just at the end of the hallway, and if she needed anything, all she had to do was call.

Ten minutes later, the screaming started.

Gemma broke into a run. The high, piercing shrieks were turning her blood cold. When she burst into Room 3C, she could hardly believe her eyes.

The room itself looked as if it had been ransacked by a burglar. The old woman was sitting in a chair, positioned haphazardly on one side.

When Gemma had left her, she had been tucked up in

bed. Normally, this would not have been a big deal, but she knew that the lady had suffered a number of strokes, which had weakened her left side to the point of near-paralysis. She also had a broken right hip, which had been surgically repaired three days before. There was no way imaginable that she could have gotten herself out of bed, let alone walked across the room and deposited herself in a chair. It was simply impossible...

...and yet there it was, as plain as day. Quickly, her mind raced to find a rational explanation for what had just happened. No matter how she turned the situation over in her mind, trying to see it from all angles, she kept on drawing a blank. It was inconceivable that the old lady could have crossed the room herself; nor could somebody else have entered the room and moved her, because if they had, Gemma would have seen them from her position at the end of the hallway.

The sheets and blankets had been hurled from the bed, with what looked like a great deal of force.

"How did you get into the chair?" Gemma asked, aghast.

"He dragged me!"

From the look on the old woman's face, Gemma suddenly felt sure that she knew exactly who 'He' was. Nevertheless, her suspicions were confirmed when the frightened lady said that it was "the army man."

Despite being all too aware of Room 3C's scary

reputation, and being able to sense an oppressive atmosphere inside it, Gemma was also a logical thinker, and knew that sometimes these things were little more than stories, made up to frighten new members of the team.

This, on the other hand, was a little harder to explain away. She began to ask around. By all accounts, this was the first time that anybody — patient or staff — had ever reported seeing the apparition of a soldier in 3C.

A few days later, another room became available. The staff wasted no time in moving the occupant of Room 3C out. Gemma and one of her colleagues were in the now-empty 3C, collecting up the old lady's belongings and getting ready to take them across to her new room.

Gemma began gathering up what clothing and other personal possessions surrounded the bed, while her companion went into the bathroom to pick up toiletries. Suddenly, there came the sound of a loud slap from inside the bathroom. Gemma looked up in surprise as her colleague emerged, a look of shock on her face...and a bright red mark discoloring one cheek.

On closer inspection, it became clear that the mark was actually a hand print.

Something plainly did not want them to be inside that room. Deciding that discretion was the better part of valor, they quickly left the room and locked the door behind them.

Room 3C stayed that way for the next few weeks, locked

and deserted. When it finally came time to open the room up again, the staff were more than a little disconcerted to find that the one and only window had been broken...from the *inside*.

"There's nothing wrong with the rest of the building," Gemma points out, "it's just that one room. You walk in there, and the atmosphere hits you like a sledgehammer. Looking back with the benefit of hindsight, there's nothing strange about the rest of the building...just Room 3C."

As time went on, Gemma found herself intrigued by the identity of the mysterious soldier. Just who, exactly, had he been? She delved into the records of the building itself and the ground that it had been built on, wondering whether an army base had once occupied the site — but no, it had no military history or significance whatsoever. Perhaps, then, the soldier was the ghost of a man who had once been a resident there, and had remained behind in spirit form after his death. Whatever the reason for his lingering and whoever he was, one thing was for sure: he was an angry soul indeed.

Gemma no longer works there, but still keeps in touch with some of her friends and former colleagues. At the time of writing, Room 3C had remained locked for the past three years, and (short of a dire emergency) shows no signs of ever being opened up for residential use again. This is probably a wise move on their part, for the room already has an occupant — and he is not a man that tolerates intrusion.

Gemma spent nine years working at a care home which served as an enhanced dementia unit, looking after those who are afflicted with one of the cruelest diseases imaginable. The work was physically demanding (she was beaten black and blue by aggressive residents on more than one occasion) but infinitely rewarding in an emotional sense. Such carers are truly unsung heroes of the healthcare field, doing a thankless, often dangerous job, and showing great compassion toward their fellow men and women; in fact, rather than refer to it as a job, it might be fairer to say that this is nothing less than a calling, and thankfully there are those kind and courageous souls who are willing to answer that call.

No shortage of strange things happened in that care home, often centered upon the rooms of those who had recently died. The call bells had a habit of ringing themselves, for example. Gemma experienced this personally in Room 37, whose previous occupant had died unexpectedly a couple of days before. The undertakers came and removed her body, but the family of the deceased woman had not yet stopped by to collect her personal belongings.

She was working a night shift, which was when unusual occurrences were most common. The call bell began to sound, coming from the now-empty room — which was also locked.

Thanks to her having been seen reading books about the paranormal, Gemma's interest in phenomena such as this was well-known among her colleagues, none of whom were willing to go and check the unoccupied room for themselves. She went without hesitation, unlocking the door and stepping inside. All was in place. The sensor mat, a pressure-sensing device which was set to alarm whenever somebody stepped on it, was plugged in and switched on at the side of the bed. This was a safety measure, as the former occupant of the room had been prone to falling out of bed. It had been activated, which should have been impossible without there being a flesh and blood person in the room to stand on it.

Ever the pragmatist, Gemma unplugged the sensor mat and took it into several other rooms over the course of the night, determined to rule out the possibility of an electrical malfunction. The mat remained obstinately silent everywhere but the deceased lady's room. She was unable to debunk the issue as an equipment problem.

Whenever a paranormal investigator is called in to investigate such claims, one of the first things they will do is look into the history of the location itself. Many hauntings occur not because of the building as it is seen today, but rather, something that occurred on the ground upon which it stands. In the case of this particular care home, it now occupied a stretch of land that was once home to a maternity hospital. Could that have played a role in the strange activity which took place there, including electric kettles switching themselves on, and doors slamming themselves shut in the middle of the night? I would suspect so.

Some supporting evidence for this theory comes in the form of crying babies, something that the staff members heard quite often. "Who's got a baby in *here?*" they would ask. Needless to say, no baby was ever found. This was likely a residual phenomenon, a psychic holdover from the days in which babies were regularly birthed and cared for at the maternity hospital.

Sightings of apparitions were also not unusual. Nothing spectacular, or frightening — just ordinary-looking people, seen in rooms which subsequently turned out to be empty.

Gemma's area of specialization was end of life care, one of the most difficult and yet equally rewarding aspects of the healthcare profession. As with so many other palliative care providers, she noticed a distinct upswing in the frequency and intensity of paranormal activity when a resident was about to die.

One patient in particular left an unforgettable impact on her. This gentleman had been undergoing end of life care for the past two weeks. The only relief from his pain came in the form of heavy-duty intravenous narcotics, which were continuously titrated with computerized precision by an infusion pump, set to administer very specific amounts of medication over a given period of time. He now existed in a semi-comatose state, his needs completely taken care of by the carers.

All of the staff knew, from the raspy rattle of his breathing, that this man wasn't long for this world. Tragically, he had no family visitors; his children now lived overseas, and he was basically all alone. Recognizing the fact that his time was fast coming to an end, Gemma told her colleagues that she was going to sit with him while he passed. Nobody should ever have to die alone, and even if he never woke up, she wanted to make sure that he had companionship when he drew his last breath; one last simple act of human kindness.

Sitting down in a chair at his bedside, Gemma took the man's limp hand and held it in her own. She had been working long shifts that week, and it wasn't long before she drifted off to sleep.

She was awoken with a start by the feeling of a hand tugging sharply on her tunic. Opening her eyes, she expected to find one of the carers bringing her a cup of tea or coffee — but there was nobody there.

Blinking the sleep from her eyes, she sat up and looked toward the bed. As if on cue, the old man drew a final, agonal breath, and then stopped breathing. His body became limp as the life left it. Gemma gave his hand one last squeeze, an acknowledgment of the precious time they had just shared with one another.

Looking back on the experience now, she believes that whoever it was that had woken her up was trying to tell her something along the lines of: *Hey, you've taken good care of him up until now. Don't sleep through the last few seconds.*

It's also possible that this was the spirit of the departed man himself. A number of psychic mediums tell us that the spirit can leave the body prior to its actual death, so it is not out of the question to think that he himself was saying goodbye to Gemma on his way out.

Nor is this the only strange occurrence that she has witnessed at the bedside of a dying person. Gemma has seen curtains blow outward just as a dying breath was taken, despite there having been no windows open in the room at the time.

There is no shortage of anecdotal evidence to support the possibility of people knowing that they are about to die. This is something that many medical providers and carers have told me over the years. Gemma had her own experience with that, when a female resident once told her very cheerfully: "I'm going to die today, Gemma!"

"Don't be silly," she laughed, jokingly dismissing it with a wave of her hand. "That would create far too much paperwork for me!"

The old lady chuckled, and went on her way. She had been heading for the restroom. *She's been in there a long time,* Gemma thought to herself a few minutes later, looking up at the clock. *I'd better go and check on her.*

When she did, Gemma found that she had passed away while sitting on the toilet.

She had *known*.

Many terminally-ill patients claim to see the spirits of departed family members as they approach their last moments. This happened to my own mother, who died of cancer in a British hospice; when I asked, I was told by the care staff without the slightest hint of reservation that she had been holding conversations with her parents in the hours before her passing.

It is tempting to think that this is nothing more than the brain playing tricks, or perhaps some sort of defense mechanism that is intended to help ease the nearly-deceased through what can sometimes be a difficult and traumatic process; however, the very objective phenomena that often accompanies these visits, makes that argument ring hollow.

And what, then, are we to make of the lucid intervals which are also very well-described by those who sit vigil at the bedsides of the dying? Even after months — sometimes *years* — of suffering from diminished or absent mentation, there are reports of patients waking up immediately before dying. They tend to be completely 'with it,' in mental terms, and will sometimes describe seeing into some other realm, or talking to people that nobody else present in the room can see. It is as if, for one bright, shining moment, some kind of veil is lifted, and the disease processes which were ravaging the dying person's body are somehow overcome by something greater. Then, they die.

"People tend to brush these experiences off too easily, without questioning them," opines Gemma, having seen a great deal of this sort of thing during her years in the caring profession. Deathbed sightings of deceased loved ones are particularly common, she says, and often have much more credibility than some people would believe. Perhaps most importantly, they usually bring great comfort to the sufferer.

Why does Gemma believe that so many care homes are haunted?

"Carers bond emotionally with the people we look after," she says. "While we often assume that people just cross over when they die, what if there's nobody there to meet them straight away? Is it so difficult to believe that their spirit might just hang around those who they have bonded with? They're going to linger until whatever unfinished business they have is taken care of."

CHAPTER FOUR
Code Blue

Angela's first job in the healthcare field was working in a hospital as a registration clerk. Her job was to take down the personal demographics of newly-arrived patients — their name, date of birth, social security number, and so forth — and enter them into the computer system. It may not be a glamorous job, but it is an absolutely essential one. Without the registration process, keeping track of patients (and their associated medical records) would be next to impossible.

One of her responsibilities was meeting the arriving ambulance crews, and it wasn't long before Angela became very familiar with the many faces of death, whether it arrived in the form of an illness, or multiple traumatic injuries.

She has had a life-long interest in the paranormal; her first personal encounter with it took place when she was just six years old. Angela had been admitted to the hospital in order to have her tonsils removed.

Unfortunately, the anesthesiologist administered a little too much of the sedative that was intended to render her unconscious. Her heart stopped in the middle of the procedure; in fact, Angela went into cardiac arrest no less than three times, forcing the surgical team to perform CPR in order to bring her back. Incredibly, enough blood was driven to her brain to keep it functioning, because when she regained consciousness, Angela remembered much of what had happened to her on the operating table.

She also began to see spirits.

Her talent for perceiving them only grew stronger as she got older. Now in her forties, Angela sees them on a regular basis. She has applied her abilities to conducting paranormal field research, helping those out those live in haunted houses.

When she began working at the hospital, it didn't take long for Angela's psychic sensitivity to begin encroaching on her everyday job.

One night, Angela was working at the emergency department registration desk when a Jane Doe was brought in by paramedics. She hurried toward the room, thinking that she could collect the patient's driver's license or some other form of ID from her purse while the medical staff did their thing.

The patient lying on the wheeled gurney was an old lady. Angela estimated her age at around ninety. She was stick-thin and appeared to be extremely frail. Her eyelids fluttered open weakly, revealing a pair of the most beautiful blue eyes that Angela had ever seen.

She locked eyes with Angela, reached out, and grabbed her hand.

"*Help me,*" she begged, her voice full of quiet desperation.

Angela was at a loss. What was she — a registration clerk — supposed to do, in order to help a dying woman? She wasn't a doctor or a nurse...she worked in *administration.*

It suddenly dawned on her that there was at least one thing that she could do...she could help take away some of the old lady's fear and loneliness. Giving her hand a reassuring squeeze, Angela smiled and kept a firm grip on it all the way to the emergency room.

That seemed to help comfort her a little, but before long, she was struggling to breathe. Rather than watch her fight for air any longer, one of the nurses fetched a bag-valve mask, and after placing the clear plastic mask over the patient's nose and mouth and obtaining a tight seal, began to slowly, purposefully squeeze air into the old woman's gasping lungs.

Angela kept holding her hand. She did that for as long

as she could, until it became clear that her presence was physically impeding the medical team, who needed to get free access to all sides of the patient. Her breathing problem was getting worse, and respiratory arrest was beginning to look inevitable.

Wanting to remain useful, Angela snatched up the old lady's purse and hurried out of the room, heading for the admission desk. Passing the unit secretary, she sat down in front of the computer. Retrieving the patient's ID, she entered it into the admissions database.

When she returned to the room a few moments later, Angela was surprised to find that the hallway outside was full of people. The way in which these newcomers were all lined up seemed a little peculiar.

Where on Earth did all these people come from?

Hospital policy clearly forbade gatherings such as this. It was a safety hazard, and risked slowing down the movements of the doctors, nurses, and techs as they came and went from the patient's bedside. Why had the unit secretary flouted the rules by allowing these family members to congregate in the corridor like that?

Angela paused for a moment to take a good look at them. The first thing that struck her was that all of them were elderly. Two of the visitors appeared to be in deep conversation.

"She was such a nice woman," one of them said, shaking his head sadly.

"That's okay," replied the lady standing next to him. "She'll be with us soon…"

At that moment, time itself seemed to slow down. Angela felt as though things were moving in slow-motion. Walking past the impromptu gathering, she returned the patient's purse, placing it gently on the stand at her bedside. The only other person in the ED room was a nurse named Robin, yet Angela could suddenly sense somebody moving past her side; she could feel breath against the side of her face, and the definite movement of her hair as if it was caught in a draft.

Then a voice whispered into her ear: *She's going to die.*

Angela almost jumped out of her own skin; so sudden and unexpected was the spirit voice, she was taken completely by surprise. She spun around, looking across the room at Robin.

"Did you say something?" she asked the nurse.

"No, hon." Robin shook her head. "Why, do you need something?"

"I...just thought I heard somebody say something to me."

The nurse favored her with a slightly odd look, and went back to caring for her patient. Angela left the room. The entire throng of visitors — all twelve of them — were gone. She didn't think much of it at the time, simply assuming that the unit secretary had cleared the group out and asked them to go and sit in the lobby. Encountering the secretary at the registration desk, Angela realized that she couldn't see any of the elderly people sitting in the lobby, and asked her where they had all gone.

"What people?" the secretary asked, sounding confused.

"You didn't see a group of people...*twelve* people...standing in the hallway outside the patient's room just now?" Angela could scarcely believe it. "How could you fail to notice that?"

"I don't know what you're talking about. That patient hasn't had a single visitor since she got here..."

Angela's jaw gaped. The penny suddenly dropped. "They've come to take her to Heaven," she said softly, talking to herself. It was the only explanation that made a lick of sense.

Yet there had been nothing out of the ordinary about the

twelve, nothing ghostly or ethereal. They had looked every bit as solid and real as any flesh-and-blood human being did.

But they had been spirits.

Before the unit secretary could react, a voice came over the public address system. "Code Blue. Code Blue in the Emergency Department."

Code Blue was the hospital term for a patient going into cardiac arrest. Both women knew exactly who it was that had just died. As one, they turned to look in the direction of the old lady's room.

Angela now understood just who the twelve visitors had been: an ethereal welcoming committee of sorts, come to accompany the dying old lady from this world into the next. She was glad that the woman was now free from her earthly pains and worries, but at the same time, Angela felt more than a little frustrated that she had been asked for help, and hadn't been able to do anything more than simply hold her hand for a short time before she died.

When she sat back down at her desk and tried to get on with business as usual, Angela couldn't stop one thought from running around and around inside her head: *Why me?* Why had she been the one to bear witness to it all? None of the actual caregivers had seen the spirits, as far as she could tell. Maybe they lacked the psychic ability to do so, or maybe they were just so completely focused on the task at hand — trying to save the elderly woman who was dying right there in front of them.

Pondering the situation afterward, with the benefits of hindsight, Angela could only hope that she had done her part in helping the woman transition from this life to the next.

CHAPTER FIVE
The Hanging

In the United States, it's called the Emergency Department, or E.D. The British equivalent is known as A&E — Accident and Emergency.

No matter what it may be called, this part of a hospital is the tip of the spear; it is the department which will handle any type of emergency, ranging from a cut finger to multiple gunshot wounds, and everything in between.

It tends to be the opinion of those who work there that the word 'emergency' is usually grossly misused. To a seasoned medical professional, in order for something to qualify as an emergency, it has to be a potentially life-threatening (or at the very least, limb-threatening) situation. Yet what members of the public generally consider to be an emergency is...well, literally *anything* that they, personally, believe to be one: Long-standing aches and pains, which suddenly seem to take on a heightened level of importance at three o'clock in the morning; the unpleasant consequences of a night of heavy binge-drinking finally catching up with the drinker; or perhaps some poor soul's worries become too much for them to bear, resulting in a cry for help...or something worse.

Some of the reasons are valid emergencies. Many are not, which goes some way toward explaining why Accident and Emergency Departments across the United Kingdom are buckling under the sheer volume of patients that are coming through their doors.

For the most part, Glynis liked working as a nurse in A&E. It was a challenging and fast-paced job, and one that gave her the opportunity to do a lot of good in the world.

It was also extremely hard work.

This particular shift had been a long and difficult one. When she glanced up at the clock, Glynis was relieved to see that it was coming to an end. The influx of patients had never even seemed to slow down, let alone stop. There were still around fifty of them in the waiting room, still waiting to be seen.

This wasn't the hospital she usually worked at. Glynis was on secondment here, gaining experience in the emergency setting. The staff made a great team, always looking out for one another and helping each other shoulder what was often a heavy workload.

As the hands on the clock crept closer toward the hour, she began to think about wrapping things up and making her exit.

Then the phone rang.

Not just any phone. This was the red emergency phone, which meant that an ambulance was coming in with a high-priority patient.

"What's coming in?" Glynis asked the colleague who had answered the phone.

"Hanging," she said tersely. "A young lad. Found out in the woods, hanging from a tree. From the sound of it, things are pretty grim."

All thoughts of leaving were now gone. Glynis didn't have to be told that the proper thing to do was to stay and help her team-mates as they struggled to snatch the patient back from the jaws of death.

She pulled on a fresh pair of latex-free gloves and set to work. The advance notice meant that there were a few minutes to prepare. A hanging almost certainly meant that a resuscitation attempt would soon be taking place. That, in turn, meant all hands on deck. Most of the A&E staff would need to pitch in.

Moments later, the paramedic crew came in through the ambulance entry doors, wheeling in their patient on a stretcher. One of them was performing chest compressions, doing their best to keep blood flowing to the young man's vital organs. If he was to have even the slightest chance at survival, then his brain, heart, liver, and kidneys would need to remain as undamaged as possible.

The resuscitation team were assembled and waiting in the resus bay, ready to receive their patient. From the first moment she saw him, Glynis knew that the outcome for this young man looked poor. The remnants of a makeshift noose were still tied around his neck. His body showed no signs of life, and from the pallid, mottled color of the skin, he had been hanging for quite some time. The only movement came in the form of his arms and legs jerking and flopping as the emergency medical technician and paramedic carried out cardio-pulmonary resuscitation (CPR).

Perhaps most ominously of all, Glynis could see what looked like an ethereal silver cord rising up out of the young man's chest. The cord appeared to have been snapped off partway along its length. Usually, when she saw such a thing, the person's spirit was visible at the other end of the cord, which anchored it to their physical body. Such a patient might have a chance of surviving, but with the spirit being completely absent…

For just a moment, Glynis could sense another presence

in the room. Glancing across the bed, she caught sight of a woman standing there silently, just watching the proceedings. She had long black hair, and wore a long, flowing white dress that made her look more than a little like somebody from a different time.

It took the attending emergency physician no more than a few seconds to determine that the tragic young man was beyond all hope of resuscitation; he had simply been dead for too long. With an exasperated sigh, the doctor pronounced the patient deceased, and looked up at the clock in order to record an official time of death.

The lady in the white dress had disappeared.

In such instances as this, the body is interfered with as little as possible. Intravenous lines, EKG electrodes, and breathing tubes are all left in place, usually as a professional courtesy to the coroner.

Reluctantly, the resus team dispersed, going back to whatever they had been doing before the ambulance had arrived. Glynis stood there for a while, lost in her own thoughts. The poor young man's eyes were red and swollen, the blood vessels having burst under the pressure of strangulation. She was struck by how handsome he must have been, before his untimely death.

Finally, it came time for Glynis to help remove his clothes. As she folded the clothes, she went through his pockets methodically, removing any personal effects and putting them aside for his next of kin to claim. In one, she found a crumpled piece of paper. Unfolding it carefully, Glynis smoothed it out. What was written there broke her heart.

I want to be with my mum.

So that was it, she realized. The poor boy had lost his mother, and hadn't been able to go on without her.

Suddenly, the aroma of strong perfume flooded the room. She had the unmistakable sense that somebody was standing directly behind her. Glynis turned, and found the dark-haired lady looking back at her.

He couldn't cope without me, the apparition told her. *Don't judge him. He wanted to be with me.*

Judgment was the last thing on the nurse's mind. This wasn't the first time she had encountered a patient having taken their own life, and it certainly would not be the last. Each of them had their own reasons for doing what they did, and who was she to cast judgment on them?

As quickly as the lady in white had appeared, she was gone again. The smell of perfume was gone too.

Glynis went back to work. There happened to be a nursing student on shift that day. The student was somewhat squeamish, which was understandable considering the fact that she hadn't been exposed to death before. Glynis was all too aware from personal experience that becoming comfortable around the dead and dying was an essential part of the nursing profession. Rather than letting the student remain in her comfort zone, Glynis directed her to clear the space around the young man's body, but without touching the body itself. She then left the room, wanting to find out if any of the patient's relatives had shown up at the hospital yet.

None had. When she returned to the nursing student once more, the scent of perfume was back. Leaning over the young man's body, she noticed that the noose around his neck had been loosened.

"Did you do this?" she asked, recalling that she had been very clear with her instruction to not touch the body. The nursing student vehemently denied it. That left only one possibility, Glynis thought to herself, sniffing at the air: the boy's mother must have tried to release the rope. Although her spirit was nowhere to be seen, the lingering odor gave her presence away.

Mindful that the dead youth's family would probably arrive at any minute, Glynis reached out and deftly pulled the bedsheet up over his body, tucking it just under his chin. This would accomplish two things: allow his loved ones to make a positive identification of him, but also conceal the rope which was still looped around his neck.

As things turned out, she had acted not a moment too soon. From somewhere out in the corridor, there came a piercing shriek. It was the sound of agonizing shock and grief. The young man's grandmother had arrived, accompanied by his father. She had been the one that had cried out.

Once she had taken a moment to compose herself, the old lady was ushered into the room where her grandson's lifeless body lay. The atmosphere was hushed and reverent, broken only by the sound of her choking back sobs.

"Why?" she asked, shaking her head. "He had such a bright future ahead of him..."

What could Glynis say to comfort her? The poor woman's life had just been torn apart. There were no words to make that better. All the nurse could do was to offer her heartfelt sympathies, and allow her natural compassion and empathy to shine through.

"Can I hold his hand?" the grandmother wanted to know. Gingerly, she reached out and touched her grandson's hand. In what must have felt like one final blow on a day already filled with more heartbreak than anybody should be asked to bear, Glynis was forced to tell her that she could not touch him…that *nobody*, other than one single, designated nurse, could touch him, until the coroner had completed their investigation and officially declared a cause of death.

The young man's father cleared his throat. "Did he…did he leave a note?" he asked quietly. Glynis admitted that he had. Forestalling what was almost sure to be a request to see it, she went on to explain that the note would have to go directly to the coroner, along with the rest of his son's personal effects. They would be returned to his next of kin following the release of a verdict, after which funeral arrangements could be made.

He nodded, clearly upset but seeming to understand and accept the situation for what it was.

"His mum died," the man explained, looking down at his son with eyes that were full of tears. "The poor lad just couldn't get over it. He had a breakdown because he couldn't live without her."

The boy's father stopped for a moment, seeming to gaze

off into the distance. Finally, he said, "That's strange. I'd swear that I smelled her perfume just now…"

Glynis was wise enough to remain quiet. After all, she reasoned, what was she going to say? "Oh yes, the spirit of his mother was here earlier on, and now she's back. I saw her." The father and grandmother would think she had gone insane.

She did as much as possible to comfort the two grieving family members. As the pair of them walked out of the hospital that night, arm in arm, Glynis knew that this was a shift she would never forget. All hints of perfume were now gone, and the spirit of the boy's mother appeared to have gone with it.

For the next two months, the grieving father visited the A & E department regularly, bringing biscuits and flowers as gifts for the nursing staff. Finally, the visits trailed off and stopped. Glynis assumed that he had begun to focus on other things, and was hopefully starting to put his terrible loss behind him.

Two years later, an ambulance crew brought a fifty-year-old male in full cardiac arrest into the A & E. As soon as she saw his face, Glynis realized that she recognized the man — it was the dead boy's father.

Now it was his turn to be placed into her care.

Glynis treated him with every bit as much respect as she had shown to his son. Although the dark-haired lady in white did not put in an appearance this time, the same, ever-present fragrance was back, and this time it was stronger than ever.

The spirit of a man appeared. Glynis would learn later that this was the dead man's brother, coming back to help ease his passage into the next life.

Glynis could only hope that now that he was reunited with his wife and son once more, the dead man's spirit would finally find the peace that had been beyond his reach for the last two years of his life.

CHAPTER SIX

The Offices of Death

With a husband who was too sick to work, nurse Glynis and her family unexpectedly found themselves in dire financial straits. She was now the sole breadwinner, and wasted no time in going to the Job Center to see what was on offer.

The first job that seemed suitable was working as an auxiliary on a specialized ward for the elderly. Her mother-in-law graciously agreed to look after the children while she went to work, and warned Glynis in a good-natured way that she would soon find herself starting to see dead people.

I already do, Glynis smiled to herself. As a psychic sensitive working in the field of healthcare, it was nothing short of inevitable that she would find herself encountering the spirits of the dead from time to time. It wasn't something she talked about publicly. After all, she didn't want anybody thinking that she was a little bit cuckoo. Yet she also knew that she wasn't the only nurse who saw ghosts.

Glynis had possessed this ability ever since she was a girl. Even all these years later, she could still vividly remember the day of her grandfather's funeral as if it had happened yesterday. As he lay there in his coffin, looking as if he was sleeping peacefully, Glynis could see a thin silver cord extending up out of his chest. It connected him to a nebulous mist that hung in the air directly above him — a mist that nobody else seemed to be able to see.

As she bent over the side of the coffin to plant a kiss on his cheek, Glynis heard her grandfather's voice speaking to her telepathically. *Look after your mum,* he told her, as clearly as if he had uttered the words when he was still alive. For the eleven-year-old, it was the first experience that truly opened her eyes to the existence of the spirit world.

Just a few days afterward, Glynis's father left her mother in order to be with another woman, causing his estranged wife to have a full-blown nervous breakdown from which she would never recover, resulting in her being admitted to a psychiatric facility.

During her first day on the geriatric ward, Glynis found that she could smell the aroma of lilies at various different spots. This was more than a little odd because there were none of the flowers to be found anywhere on the ward. She knew that this was an odor which some people associated with the presence of death.

Sure enough, her first assigned task was to assist another nurse with what was called 'the offices of death' on a newly-deceased patient. This involved washing the body of the dead person, dressing it in fresh clothes, cleaning it up, and generally making it presentable prior to the arrival of the family members.

"I'm going to go and get some fresh towels," the other nurse said, stepping out of the room. As she went, she called over her shoulder that Glynis was to brush the dead woman's hair and begin to clean her fingernails.

Glynis took a seat at the side of the bed. Picking up a nail file, she raised the woman's hand. It was cool but not yet cold, for she hadn't been dead for very long.

Suddenly, the lilies were back, and this time, the smell was stronger than ever. Only then did Glynis notice that a nurse was standing on the opposite side of the bed, looking directly across the body at her. The door to the room had not been opened, and the other nurse hadn't made a sound.

The new arrival had dark hair and brown eyes, two details that Glynis clearly remembers today, many years after the encounter. She wore an old-fashioned gray dress, with a white pinafore over the top of it. On her chest was a red cross, the universal symbol of healthcare.

"Hello," Glynis greeted the other nurse, who did not deign to reply. The two nurses gazed calmly at one another.

Glynis now knew that whoever her counterpart was, she was no flesh-and-blood person. Conscious of the fact that time was moving on, she went back to caring for the dead woman's nails.

When she looked up again, a few moments later, the phantom nurse had disappeared.

The nurse she had been assigned to help out came back into the room, and immediately wrinkled her nose. "She's been then," she said, sniffing the lily-scented air.

"Yes, she has," Glynis agreed, a wry smile playing upon her lips. Many nurses accept the existence of ghosts and spirits without even giving the matter a second thought, perhaps because so many of them have such inexplicable encounters while caring for dying patients. Just to be sure, however, she asked Glynis to describe what the phantom nurse had looked like.

"That's our gray lady," the nurse nodded. "She usually comes around when a patient passes. Isn't it strange that you saw her on your very first day here?"

Rather than being afraid, Glynis found the encounter to be a comforting and intriguing experience. The Gray Lady hadn't projected any negativity or harmful intent whatsoever; if anything, she seemed to be keeping a watchful eye on the newly-deceased patient and the new nurse on the ward.

"Do you know who she is?" Glynis asked, her curiosity getting the better of her. The other nurse shook her head.

"No. We haven't any idea. But you aren't the first nurse to see her, and I suspect you won't be the last either."

The two nurses finished taking care of their patient. Glynis wasn't willing to give up quite so easily.

One day, I will find out who that nurse is, if it's the last thing I do.

Several months passed uneventfully. Glynis had settled into her role on the geriatric ward comfortably, building a rapport with the patients and their family members, due to her compassionate bedside manner and excellent nursing skills.

One day, she was making the rounds in the middle of the day, and handing out afternoon tea — that most British of hospital traditions. As she was passing bed number four, she felt what can only be described as a 'cobwebby' feeling — this sensation, which is experienced by many of those with psychic sensitivity, is said to feel somewhat akin to walking into an enormous spider's web, and having the strands tickle one's skin. It usually indicates the presence of a spirit entity.

Glynis was already aware that the patient in that particular bed was about to pass away, having already gone into a state of rapid decline. For that reason, she wasn't taken entirely by surprise when she saw the Gray Lady sitting there, at the patient's bedside.

At the time of their first meeting, the phantom nurse had barely acknowledged Glynis's presence. It had been almost as if the Gray Lady had been sizing her up, silently judging her. Now, it seemed that whatever test had been set, Glynis must have passed it with flying colors, because this time the spirit entity turned around and offered her a friendly smile.

An instant later, the Gray Lady had disappeared. When Glynis reached the bedside, she discovered that the patient had passed away…and there was that strong smell of lilies once more.

Glynis subsequently left the geriatric ward behind, in order to further her training as a Registered General Nurse. No matter where she worked and studied, she continued to encounter spirits of many different varieties. It wasn't something she mentioned to people, for the most part; telling people that you see ghosts is rarely considered to be a good career move, after all.

Later, now a fully qualified nurse, she returned to the same ward at her former hospital.

Early one morning, she found herself making the seven o'clock drug round, helping patients to take their prescribed medications. One of the patients, an elderly gentleman, shuffled over to Glynis and asked her to thank 'that matron' for sitting with him and holding his hand the night before.

Matron? There *wasn't* a matron on the ward. Glynis asked him to describe the nurse that had comforted him. He spoke of a woman wearing a gray dress, with a while pinafore over the top of it…a pinafore that was emblazoned with a red cross. She had smelled, he told her, of flowers…

The gentleman had been admitted to the hospital in order to receive a bronchoscopy — a procedure which involves inserting a camera down into the lungs — after he had begun coughing up blood.

"How are you feeling, Mr. Smith?" Glynis asked him.

"Fine," he smiled cheerfully. "I'm as fit as a fiddle!"

Although she returned his smile encouragingly, something about the incident struck Glynis as being rather odd. If Mr. Smith really *was* in good health, he should never have received a bedside visit from the Gray Lady.

She got her answer — and a most unwelcome answer it was — later that afternoon. A little after two o'clock, Mr. Smith unexpectedly suffered a sudden cardiac arrest. Despite their best efforts, the doctors and nursing staff were unable to save him.

An autopsy would reveal that Mr. Smith had been suffering from an advanced and highly aggressive form of lung cancer. Although none of his care providers had known that yet, the Gray Lady most certainly had.

Now, more than ever, Glynis wanted to know the identity of this mysterious benefactor. She began to delve into the history of the hospital, and soon came to the conclusion that the phantom nurse was most likely none other than Miss Elizabeth Sinclair White, who had been appointed both Commandant and Matron during the First World War. One can only imagine just how many terribly wounded soldiers, sailors, and airmen were placed under her care during those terrible years of bloodshed and carnage on the Western Front.

For Glynis, her fellow nurses, and for their countless patients, the comforting presence of the lady in gray, truly was a gift from the other side.

CHAPTER SEVEN
The Matron's Dog

The year was 1978, and Glynis had just completed her training to become a fully-qualified nurse. Not long afterward, she went to work at a hospital which specialized in the care of patients suffering from mental health disorders.

She hadn't been there long before she realized that this was not a particularly endearing place to work. The building itself had seen better days. The rooms and corridors were painted in the sort of drab color scheme that would have been better suited to a military barracks than a place of healing.

I don't know if this place is haunted, Glynis thought to herself on her first day of employment there, *but if it isn't, I'll be shocked.*

The hospital itself had a decidedly colorful history. Built in 1904, it had originally been used for the care — and isolation — of those afflicted with highly-infectious diseases. Some fifty years later, it was repurposed in order to accommodate the mentally ill. (Six years after Glynis first went to work there, it would be demolished, in order to make way for a newer facility, one that was dedicated to the care of psychiatric patients).

The duty of caring for such patients is not for the faint of heart. The hospital walls echoed day and night with the screams, howls, and anguished sobs of the men and women who felt themselves to be trapped inside, many with no hope of a cure or reprieve. This, in turn, often led to violent outbursts. Many a nurse was spat on, punched, kicked, or bitten by those who were in their care. So constant was the verbal abuse, in fact, that Glynis finally learned to tune it out and just get on with the job as best she could.

For her first night shift, Glynis had been assigned to Ward Three, which was to be found at the far end of a very long hallway. Ward Three was home to six female patients, all of whom had some degree of dementia, often combined with other mental health concerns. Six might not sound like a large number of patients to occupy a ward, but each one of them was difficult to handle in some way, for they all presented their own unique challenges…and Glynis was to be their only care provider.

The night seemed to last forever. Outside, the wind was howling, sometimes so forcefully that parts of the building shook. Every so often, a loud *thud* would cause her to jolt upright in alarm — even when she learned that this was merely the sound of a bat slamming into the window, the unexpected sound set her nerves on edge.

A few hours into her shift, Glynis looked up from her work and noticed something strange. One of the patients, a lady that we shall refer to as Sarah, was surrounded by a group of twinkling lights. As quickly as they had appeared, the lights were gone again.

Like any good nurse, Glynis had taken the time to familiarize herself with her patients' medical records and assessment history. Sarah's had made for very unpleasant reading, as her story was a tragic and heartbreaking one.

When she was a young woman, Sarah had been the victim of a sexual assault. As if that wasn't horrific enough, she had become pregnant after the attack; the baby had been taken aware from her shortly after it had been born, and poor Sarah had suffered a severe mental and emotional breakdown because of it. Even many years afterward, Sarah still wept inconsolably at the thought of her lost baby — and who could possibly blame her?

Through the process of trial and error, nursing staff at the hospital had learned that one thing, and one thing only, was capable of keeping Sarah mollified: a child's doll, which she had christened 'Daisy.'

On this particularly night, Sarah was restless and upset. Intrigued by the lights she had seen dancing all around her, Glynis went to check on her patient. Sometimes, all it took in order to calm somebody down was to sit with them and hold their hand, talking to them in a soothing, compassionate tone of voice. It was something that Glynis had a gift for, and would come in handy many times during her nursing career.

Glynis had just taken a seat at Sarah's bedside, and was about to reach for her hand to ask her what was the matter. Before she could speak, she noticed the overpowering smell of lilacs. That could mean only one thing — a spirit entity was present.

Then came the growl.

She looked down. Sitting on the floor next to the bed was a dog. The German Shepherd wasn't a living creature — no animals were allowed on the hospital ward, and the concept of emotional support dogs hadn't been invented yet. Besides, Glynis had spent the last few years attuning her senses so that they could see and sense the presence of spirit entities. She knew one when she saw one.

The spirit dog didn't seem vicious; if anything, it appeared to be protecting Sarah, keeping a watchful eye on the forlorn old lady. For her part, Sarah was still inconsolable, screaming and crying despite the fact that Daisy the doll was being clutched in her hands.

Saddened that she was unable to calm Sarah down, Glynis backed away and returned to the nurse's station, where she put in a call to the charge nurse, asking that she come down to help administer a medication to help relax the distraught woman.

After a while, she realized that something about the ward seemed different. It took her a moment to realize just what that was — everything had gone quiet. Sarah had stopped crying out.

Slowly, Glynis took a few steps down the length of the ward. She noticed that there was now a stranger standing next to Sarah's bed — another nurse. At first, that didn't particularly bother her. She was brand new to the ward, after all, and she hadn't met all of her colleagues yet. But on closer inspection, it became apparent that this was no ordinary nurse.

For one thing, she had no legs.

From her nurse's hat, on down to her waist, everything about the newcomer looked normal. Where her hips should have been, however, there was nothing. Her torso appeared to be floating on empty air.

Glynis stopped in her tracks, taken aback by the arrival of this unexpected spirit visitor. The ghostly nurse was just standing there, smiling down at Sarah with a soothing look upon her face. The dog was sitting beside her, wagging its tail lazily.

Whoever this lady was, her mere presence seemed to have calmed Sarah down. By the time the charge nurse arrived to answer Glynis's call, Sarah's eyes were closed, and she was sleeping peacefully. Both the nurse and the dog had disappeared.

Glynis was burning with curiosity to find out just who the phantom nurse was, but she knew better than to ask her boss about it. It wouldn't do to be labeled as somebody who saw dead nurses on her first day on the job, after all.

Four weeks later, Glynis found herself working on the men's ward, which was home to four male patients. One of the patients, a gentleman who went by the name of Mr. Brown, was something of a character. He liked to wear a pair of brown, baggy trousers, that were usually pulled up to just below his belly button, and held up by a pair of bright red braces (suspenders, for American readers).

Mr. Brown had a very distinctive gait, which was more of a waddle than a walk.

The clock had just chimed two in the morning. Sitting at the nurses' station, Glynis heard the sound of that by-now familiar waddle. Looking up, she saw Mr. Brown passing by, and offered him a cheery smile. He raised a hand in acknowledgment, and kept on going, heading in the direction of the men's restroom.

Despite his age, Mr. Brown did not usually have any issues with going to the toilet by himself, so, when ten minutes had gone by and he still had not returned, Glynis was beginning to get worried. After five more minutes had passed, she walked down the ward to his bed, thinking that perhaps he had slipped past her while she was filling out paperwork.

There was a man sitting up in his bed, alright…but it wasn't Mr. Brown.

The newcomer was somebody Glynis hadn't seen before, apparently a new admission to the ward. She returned the smile he gave her, doing her best to mask the confusion she felt. Going back to the nurse's station, she waited for the charge nurse to take over for her so that she could go on her break.

"What happened to Mr. Brown?" she asked casually, suspecting that she already knew the answer.

"He died yesterday," the charge nurse replied, shaking his head sadly. "It's a shame. He was such a nice man."

"Yes," Glynis agreed. "Yes, he was…" She did not think it wise to reveal that she had just seen Mr. Brown's ghost, heading down the ward with his characteristic waddle — while his physical body was being kept in the morgue, pending a coroner's inquest.

After she left the hospital for the last time, Glynis made a point of asking one of the senior nurses if there had ever been a nurse on the ward who had brought her dog to work.

"Oh yes," the nurse had replied instantly. "That was Matron Jones. The children at the hospital always loved to play with her dog. But she passed away, many years ago…"

CHAPTER EIGHT

A Long Night

The field of pediatric care is one of the more challenging sub-specialties of the medical profession. To most people, few things are more distressing than a sick or injured child, particularly if they happen to be parents themselves. While it is true that medical professionals do grow calluses over their feelings sometimes — of necessity — the majority feel great compassion for the little ones entrusted into their hands.

Glynis didn't mind working on the children's ward. She also didn't mind working nights. When she had first started, she had imagined that they would be peaceful and quiet, when the kids had all drifted off to sleep for the night. As things turned out, nothing could have been further from the truth. Many of the kids woke up often throughout the night.

It also didn't help that the children's ward was located right next to the Accident and Emergency department, which meant that a constant influx of ambulances and walk-in patients made for a very noisy time of it.

Being psychically sensitive, Glynis sometimes saw colored lights dancing around the beds of the children. It tended to be the case that the more seriously ill a child was, the more often the lights would appear. She had always associated the light phenomena with the world of spirit. They came in all imaginable colors and shades, varying in brightness and intensity.

On this particular night, the three nurses who were on duty all had their hands full. In addition to the usual chorus of crying children, they were given a rather unpleasant surprise, which came in the form of a very sick child who needed to be admitted to the ward. The cause for alarm came about because the child was running a very high fever, and also had what is known as a *petechial rash* — two symptoms that are very suggestive of meningitis.

Meningitis is an infection of the central nervous system, more specifically the *meninges* — the layers of tissue which cover the brain and the spinal cord. When the meninges become inflamed, it becomes extremely painful for the sufferer. There are two main types of the disease: viral, and bacterial.

Viral meningitis, the more common variant, is usually survivable even if it goes untreated. The bacterial kind, on the other hand, can often be fatal, even when it is treated. In addition to being potentially life-threatening, it is also contagious, and requires healthcare providers to take additional protective measures in the form of body substance isolation equipment.

In order to minimize the risk of passing on the infection, patients with suspected meningitis are typically isolated. The hospitals of today have negative-pressure rooms intended for just this purpose, but those are relatively recent innovations. Prior to that, the children would have been placed in a side room, and treated under what were known as 'barrier nursing' conditions.

Glynis was the nurse assigned to take care of this poor little fellow. No sooner had she prepared a side room than a woman came onto the ward. She held a sickly, blond-haired boy by the hand. Drenched in sweat, he was crying out in pain and fear. His mother was frantic with worry.

"Please, may I take him?" Glynis asked, her heart going out to him. The mother's reaction took her completely by surprise.

Taking her son into her arms and clutching him tightly, she refused to let Glynis lay a finger on him. "The last time a nurse touched my son, she couldn't make him better!"

Uh oh, she thought ruefully. *Looks like it's going to be a long night…*

"I know you're worried about him," Glynis coaxed

gently, holding out her hands toward the child. "But we need to take care of your son. Please, let me look after him."

Reluctantly, the boy's mother surrendered her son into Glynis's care. She helped him get situated in the hospital bed, and after calming him down a little, slipped a needle into his arm and drew a blood sample. While far from pleasant, it was still much less painful than the spinal tap which was probably coming — that was how doctors tested for meningitis, by analyzing the spinal fluid for telltale signs of the bacteria. For her part, Glynis already knew that the boy was extremely sick. Not only was his skin practically burning up, but a series of multi-colored spirit lights had materialized, and were now circling protectively around his bed.

"Don't you hurt my brother."

Pulling the needle out of his arm, the nurse looked down to see who had spoken. She saw the apparition of a young boy staring back at her. The newcomer was blond-haired with blue eyes, the veritable spitting image of the poorly boy who lay in the bed next to him.

Not wanting to alarm the agitated mother any further, Glynis spoke to the flesh-and-blood child, instead of his incorporeal brother. "Don't worry…nothing will hurt you here. We're going to take care of you, and make you better."

His response was heartbreaking. "You didn't make my brother better..."

Ah, Glynis thought. Suddenly, the presence of the spirit boy was starting to make sense.

Things moved quickly after that. The boy's condition was indeed serious, and rapidly getting worse. The nurses went into high gear, and arranged for an emergent transfer to a children's hospital, where pediatric specialists would be on hand to provide him with definitive medical care.

Glynis accompanied him in the ambulance, doing her very best to prevent his condition from deteriorating even further. His mother was also riding in with them. Her eyes were red and puffy from all of the crying she had been doing.

"Please save my son," she practically begged. "He's all I have. I lost his twin brother to meningitis this time last year..."

Although things were touch and go for a while, the medical staff were finally able to turn things around. The young boy lost four of his toes in the process — two on each foot — but his life was saved and he regained his health. Glynis suspected that having the spirit of his deceased brother nearby, keeping a watchful eye over him, might have played a part in his recovery.

Twenty years later, Glynis was working a shift in Accident and Emergency, when a man walked in who seemed...*familiar*, somehow. While she might not have recognized him, the man certainly knew who she was.

"I remember you from twenty years ago!" he said, giving her a broad grin that was tinged with pain. "You're the nurse that took care of me when I had meningitis."

Now, the young man was at the hospital with a toe wound that had gotten infected. What were the chances of him encountering Glynis after all these years?

"I remember you too," Glynis laughed, giving him a big hug.

Suddenly, his mood turned serious. "My brother was there with me that night," he told her. "You saw him, didn't you? I could tell."

What was the point in denying it? "Yes, I saw him."

"He's been with me every day of my life. In fact, he's always with me."

Glynis knew that he was telling the truth, because there,

standing next to the front doors of A & E, stood the phantom boy, still watching over his brother more than twenty years after he had died.

CHAPTER NINE
Bed, Bath, and Beyond

Some people believe in angelic beings. Others do not. But something on which practically all of us can agree, is that the men and women who work with dying human beings are one of the closest things imaginable to angels walking the Earth. There are few nobler forms of service than that of helping our fellow souls through the final stages of life.

Emma is one such person. Working for a private company which supplied caregivers to terminally ill patients, both in medical facilities and in the comfort of their own homes, she put her heart and soul into delivering the most compassionate care that she possibly could.

One of her patients was a lady named Clara, who was in her fourth year of receiving home hospice care. Clara suffered from dementia, one of the cruelest diseases with which one can be afflicted. In a permanently catatonic state, she was unable to leave her bed. Nor could she speak.

Due to her severely debilitating disease, all of Clara's needs had to be met by healthcare workers such as Emma. It was their responsibility to prepare Clara's meals, which were one hundred percent liquid, and fortified with a stiffening agent. Once she had fed her patient, Emma then went about the task of bathing Clara, changing her clothes, and flipping her carefully on the mattress in order to prevent bed-sores. They also administered Clara's medications for her.

Clara didn't always take this lying down (no pun intended). She had a reputation for being, as Emma and her fellow carers liked to say, "a stubborn old gal." They didn't resent her for it. Given her condition — being essentially trapped inside her own body, unable to communicate, unable to take care of even the most basic of needs for herself — must have been incredibly frustrating. From time to time, that frustration expressed itself in the form of physical resistance. Clara would sometimes fight back against those who were trying to take care of her.

Clara was married, and lived with her husband, who did his best to keep things ticking along. The problem was, he was a little on the frail side himself, and so the carers made a point of helping out with a few light chores around the house whenever they could spare the time. This included putting the soiled linens in the washing machine, which was downstairs in the basement.

It wasn't long before Emma realized that the laundry was no longer being taken down to be washed. When she asked her colleagues why not, a couple of them explained — with no small degree of embarrassment — that they found the basement to be 'really eerie,' and looked for any possible reason to avoid going down there.

Emma, on the other hand, was made of sterner stuff. While she agreed with them about the basement being a little on the creepy side, it was also part of her job to make sure that the linens got washed. Whenever she was down there, the hairs on the back of Emma's neck stood on end. Despite the fact that she was alone down there, she could never quite escape the feeling of being watched, and always looked over her shoulder while she worked.

One night, Clara's husband said that he was going to take a walk around the block. Emma didn't think much of it at the time, but when the old man returned, she had the distinct feeling that something else had come back into the house with him. He was quite clearly alone, but something just felt *off*. It was difficult to put her finger on exactly what it was, but she couldn't shake the sensation.

In the past, Clara's nephew would drop by to visit her on occasion. Perhaps that was what she was picking up on. Emma searched the house from top to bottom, and found nobody.

Clara's husband sometimes used the home health care visits as an opportunity to get out of the house for a little while. Emma encouraged this, knowing that a change of scenery would be good for him, and so when he announced later that evening that he would be taking his daughter out to dinner, she waved him goodbye and set about her list of tasks for the shift.

Now that she and Clara were alone in the house, Emma went into the kitchen and set about preparing the liquid meal.

It was then that she began to hear the voices.

At first, Emma thought she must be imagining them. It sounded as if there were conversations going on, just at the edge of her hearing. Whispered voices, the actual words themselves indistinct. The house was large, built upon four different levels. Clara's room was at the top of the staircase, situated on the left. Directly across from it were two other rooms and a large bathroom. Climbing the stairs, one hand on the rail, Emma became convinced that the voices were coming from Clara's room…yet when she peeked inside, the voices immediately stopped. She saw that the old lady was lying in bed, gazing up toward the ceiling. Her lips weren't moving.

After checking all of the rooms to make sure that there

was indeed nobody else in the house, Emma sat down at the side of Clara's bed and began to feed her. The two women had developed a mealtime ritual of listening to some of Clara's favorite music while she ate. This time, however, Emma deliberately left the music off — she wanted to see if the voices would return.

The two women passed the time in companionable silence. All the while, Emma sat and listened to the sounds of the house settling, the occasional creaks and pops that are perfectly natural at night when the structure contracts and settles. She wondered if perhaps a neighbor might be playing a radio, or have the volume on their TV set cranked up, but no noise was carrying in from the outside world. There wasn't even the sound of vehicle engines driving past.

"I…want…more."

The voice took Emma by surprise. It had come from none other than Clara herself. That was no mean feat, considering the fact that she had been completely non-verbal for the past few years. The old woman looked at Emma plaintively.

"Of course you can have some more," she said, gently assisting her with drinking a few additional mouthfuls of liquid. Once she had taken in her fill, Clara's head sank back onto the pillow with a contented sigh.

Emma talked to her for a while longer, but Clara did not speak again. Nor did she do anything to give the impression that she had even understood what it was that her caregiver had been saying. If the truth be told, Emma was rather shaken by what had happened. How, after all this time, had her charge suddenly managed to speak?

She pondered the matter as she went into the kitchen and began washing up after dinner. She had heard stories about catatonic, sometimes completely comatose patients who suddenly experienced a lucid episode, but that usually happened right before…

Emma stopped dead in her tracks.

Those lucid moments typically took place right before the patient died.

Her heart racing, Emma went back upstairs to the bedroom and looked inside. Clara lay there quietly, catatonic once more. Emma was relieved to see that her chest rose and fell regularly. She had reverted to her normal baseline state, but at least Emma's fear about her dying had turned out to be unfounded.

Brushing the thought away, she went back to work. It would soon be time for Clara's bath. Emma began to gather the washcloths and soap that she knew she would need from the bathroom. She heard a voice coming from somewhere behind her, in the direction of the bedroom.

It was Clara. She was talking again. Although Emma couldn't quite make out the specific words, the old lady's voice was unmistakable. She turned around and stepped out into the hallway. Once again, something felt...*WRONG* to her.

Suddenly, from out of nowhere, a blast of icy cold air shot past her, like a train rushing by at high speed. Clara was still speaking. Emma began to walk forward, having been caught off guard for a few seconds by the unexpected coldness.

"What happened next will probably make me sound crazy," she says, looking back on the events of that night with the benefit of hindsight. "But it is what it is."

Death was waiting inside that room. She could feel it with every fiber of her being, a bone-deep conviction that apart from herself and Clara, there was another presence in the room. While it didn't feel particularly menacing, as such, Emma was absolutely certain that the unseen and uninvited visitor had come to attend to Clara.

She went over to check on her patient. Clara had fallen

quiet once more, and looked as if she might be sleeping. Emma leaned over her and made sure that she was still breathing. The atmosphere in the room was now so thick, it was almost palpable.

What was she supposed to do now? After thinking it over for a moment, Emma decided that the only thing to do was to go about her business as usual. She went back to the bathroom and fetched the supplies she had gathered for Clara's bed bath.

The sweet old lady made small grunting and moaning noises while Emma washed her. Usually, she was completely silent during her bed baths, except for those occasions when her dementia was particularly bad and she was physically resisting care.

As she went about cleaning Clara up, Emma spoke tenderly to her, telling Clara how much she meant to her, and letting her know that she would brush her hair nicely, "and make you look your best, just in case you get any visitors." All the while, Emma could feel that the presence in the room was getting stronger. When she first sensed it, the unseen being was lurking at the back of the bedroom. Now, it had changed location, moving out into the hallway beyond. Emma had her back to the doorway while she took care of

Clara, but could feel it behind her, watching everything that she did. There was no sense of threat, but she was now more certain than ever that the spirit entity had come to escort Clara on what was to be her final journey.

Once she had finished giving Clara her bed bath, Emma carefully changed her clothing and re-positioned her in the bed. She pulled the sheets over Clara, tucked her in, and dimmed the lights so that she could get a little sleep.

Stepping out into the hallway, she realized that the entity seemed to have moved again. It hadn't left. She could feel that it was still somewhere inside the house. The question was: where, exactly? Emma was starting to get a little uneasy, and it took her a moment to figure out the reason: this was starting to remind her of her own mother's death, bringing back some unpleasant memories.

She went from room to room, trying to pinpoint the spirit entity's location. It remained maddeningly elusive. Finally, she decided to address it directly. Although Emma felt a little silly talking to thin air, she couldn't really see a better option.

"Look, I know that you're here," she began, looking all around her. "I know that you have a job to do, and I promise not to interfere with that. But listen...I have to go down into the basement right now. Please, *please*, do not try to scare me. It's creepy enough down there as it is!"

Silence.

Because there was no answer, Emma could see little choice other than to go downstairs and hope for the best. Standing at the top of what was usually a dark and foreboding staircase, she reached out and flipped on the light. To her surprise, things felt different this time. While not exactly warm and friendly, as she went down the steps, Emma didn't feel the usual sense of nervousness or the unwelcome feeling of being watched. Instead, the atmosphere felt somewhat flat…almost inert.

Putting the laundry into the washing machine and firing it up, she went back upstairs. The house was quiet now, and she had little else to do but wait for Clara's husband to come home. When he did, Emma let him know that his wife had been fed, bathed, and was now sleeping. She made a note to that effect in the caretaker's log which she and the other carers shared, and left for the night.

The unseen presence was still there.

She returned to the house several days later. Checking the log book, she found that none of her colleagues had made notes about Clara having spoken again. Perhaps it had been a one-off, Emma mused; an aberration.

When she sat down at the sleeping Clara's side, Emma could sense the presence of the entity once again. It was just hanging out, like a low-level background hum that one soon got used to and mentally tuned out…but was there nonetheless.

She had been half-expecting a phone call on one of her days off, telling her that Clara had passed away in her sleep. That was the distinct feeling she had gotten from the invisible visitor. Instead, she found Clara in her usual condition, completely non-verbal.

Emma sat quietly with her for the remainder of her shift, gently stroking the old lady's hair in an attempt to give her some small measure of comfort. Clara's plight had touched her deeply, and Emma tried to imagine what life had been like for Clara when she was her own age, long before the crow's feet, wrinkles, and lines had come to her face.

Clara didn't have much of a quality of life, but her husband was still making the best of things, and Emma suspected that might have been the reason why she hadn't passed on yet. The two of them had been married for more than sixty years — longer than an entire lifetime for some people — and it was likely that Clara didn't want to leave him on his own for too long. In this day and age, where one out of two marriages ends in divorce, this kind of longevity was a relative rarity. Such closely-forged bonds are not easily broken.

It was a quiet and uneventful night. When she got up to leave at the end of her shift, Clara still hadn't stirred or spoken a word. Emma stepped out into the hallway and switched out the light. Just then, the old lady's voice came out of the darkness from behind her. She spoke only three words.

"It's almost time."

The carer paused for a moment on the top step, not wanting to look back. She could still sense the spirit's presence in the house. Whatever it was, it now felt more comforting than unnerving, and Emma left the house confident that her charge was in good hands.

As fate would have it, she would never return. She heard through the grapevine that Clara had passed away shortly after she had left. A few days later, her husband joined her.

While for many people, this would have been a cause for sorrow and tears, Emma saw things differently. The two of them were so close that he hadn't been able to survive without his wife by his side, even in such a debilitated state.

In fact, it was very likely that he really hadn't wanted to go on without her.

As for the identity of the mysterious spirit presence that she had sensed, well...that can never be determined for certain. The literature of paranormal research is replete with stories of the spirits of the dead returning in order to help ease the transition of a dying person into the next life. Sometimes this is a family member or loved one of theirs, somebody who has died and returned to act as a protector during the last few hours of life on this plane.

Psychic mediums claim that in other cases, this may be one of the soon-to-be-departed's assigned spirit guides, fulfilling their final earthly responsibility to the person they have been watching over.

And then there is the third possibility...

Practically every human culture and society throughout the annals of recorded history has had its version of an 'angel of death,' a phantom harbinger of imminent demise. Sometimes this comes in the form of a sinister supernatural herald, such as the Banshee of Irish folklore.

Said to be a female spirit, the Banshee has been reported in the form of a beautiful young woman and also that of a horrifying old hag. The legends imply that the Banshee can change its form at will. One common aspect of these stories is that the mournful specter is usually seen to be weeping. Often, the Banshee is heard to be singing a sad lament, though there are also accounts of the entity screaming and shrieking in the most demented of ways — sometimes the screams are so high-pitched that they will shatter glass windows.

The Banshee is believed to be a predictor of death, and strikes great fear and dread into those who encounter her.

Yet in the case of Clara and her husband, there was no sense of impending doom reported. The care workers reported feeling uneasy down in the basement, but that could simply have been a purely psychological phenomenon — after all, who likes to go downstairs to the basement while they're on their own in a stranger's house? Once the carers began to swap stories of how creepy and uncomfortable it felt down there, a feedback loop of sorts could have been formed, with each story reinforcing the next one.

On the other hand, Emma was absolutely convinced that there was an unseen presence in the house, usually in the vicinity of Clara. Could it be possible that what the carers were sensing was in fact this very observer, following them around as they went about the course of their duties? The spirit seemed to be a protective one, watching over Clara during her last days. It would therefore make sense that such a spirit entity might keep an eye on the healthcare workers, making sure that they were doing everything that needed to be done in order to look out for Clara.

CHAPTER TEN
Remembering Nathan

More than a hundred years old, the huge red brick manor house had been built in order to take care of society's outcasts: the elderly, the poverty-stricken, and the mentally ill.

After serving its purpose for the better part of a century, it was ignominiously shut down and abandoned. The hallways and corridors, which had once bustled with life, were now dark and silent. All of the patients and the staff members that had cared for them were gone, leaving medical records and personal belongings scattered all around.

The building was now left to its ghosts, and those who sought to find them.

Emma was fascinated with the place. She enjoyed walking the halls, immersing herself in the quiet, somber atmosphere. *If only these walls could talk*, she reflected, wandering in and out of the empty rooms which had until just a few years ago been somebody's home.

Those people had left behind mementos of their time at the manor. Here, a faded photograph was taped to a cabinet door; there, an old sweat-shirt lay discarded in the corner of a room. Signs of those who had, in some cases, lived most of their adult lives inside this place. Emma could feel the energy that had remained long after the people themselves had gone.

The manor may have been abandoned, but it was far from being truly empty.

She knew that some had wrestled with their personal demons: addiction, mental illness, and chronic disease. Countless people had also died here, breathing their last in one of the many beds that were still to be found in a number of the rooms. As a tangible reminder of that, a cemetery could still be found just outside the grounds. Its tombstones had faded after so many years of exposure to the elements, but the graveyard was otherwise neatly kept, the grass neatly trimmed and the trash picked up at regular intervals. It was a peaceful place, and Emma enjoyed the sense of tranquility she felt when walking there.

She had arranged to spend a night carrying out a paranormal investigation at the ramshackle old building. Before setting out, Emma had made a point of doing her homework, delving into the history of the location. She noted with interest that it was not the first structure to have been built on that site. A 'Poor Farm' had previously occupied that spot, until it had been torn down in order to make way for the newer facility. If you were destitute or mentally ill, and your family happened to be either unwilling or unable to take care of you, then the Poor Farm was essentially your only other option, other than living rough on the streets. It offered a structured life, with regular meals, a roof over your head, and some degree of social interaction; in return, you were expected to work on the farm from dawn until dusk.

Emma decided to select one of the residents at random from the historical records, and see whether she could connect with him in some way during her investigation. After all, she reasoned, how many men, women, and children had lived at the manor over the years, generation after generation coming and going. Perhaps some of them had not truly moved on yet…

After poring over the records, she finally settled upon a man named Nathan, who was a resident at the poor farm in the late 1800s. He died only three weeks after his arrival there, aged just 45, and was buried in the cemetery across the road.

When she arrived at the manor house, Emma had brought along as much information about Nathan as she could gather from the historical records. Her hope was that learning as much about his background as possible (including his place of birth, names of his immediate family, and important dates during his lifetime) might help her to connect with him in some way.

Unfortunately, the team investigation was so busy that night, she was unable to find the time to sit down alone and try to make contact with him. As the night wore on, Emma closed her eyes for a while, as she and her colleagues grabbed a quick power nap before the sun rose. They were staying in a guest house on the grounds, away from the main building itself.

When she awoke, it was to the sound of two people talking. While the words themselves were indistinct, one of the voices was quite clearly that of a woman. Thinking that the rest of the team had awoken before her and were already up and about, she rubbed the sleep from her eyes and went to check on them.

Her fellow investigators were still asleep. Thinking that to be rather odd, her next thought was that the other team with which they were investigating must be walking around the place. When she went to look in on them, however, it turned out that they had already left.

Then just who, she wondered, had she heard talking?

Shrugging it off, Emma made a pot of coffee and poured herself a cup, then went outside to walk the grounds. It was a cold morning, and a curtain of dense fog blanketed the manor and its surroundings. She found it hard to shake the feeling that she was in some kind of creepy movie, or an episode of *The Twilight Zone*.

She stood there for a few moments, watching as the fog bank flowed around the manor house. Every so often, a window would become visible through a clear patch, and Emma got the distinct impression that she might see a face looking back at her if she stood there long enough.

Finally, shaking her head, she walked slowly around to the front of the building. If memory served, there was a wooden bench close to the front doors. She sat down on it, her back to the manor, and gazed out into the drifting, swirling grayness. The atmosphere no longer felt scary to her; if anything, the morning now felt peaceful, and Emma relaxed on the bench, enjoying this new-found sense of peace and quiet, and the simple pleasure of hot coffee on a cold day.

After a while, she lit a cigarette. Suddenly, the sound of footsteps on the wet grass coming from somewhere behind her, told Emma that at least one of her colleagues was now awake. From the sound of it, she could tell that the footsteps had a leisurely air about them, as though their owner was sauntering casually without a care in the world.

Shawn was coming to join her for a cigarette, she assumed, not bothering to turn around and see.

Finally, the footsteps were just a few paces behind her. They stopped. "Good morning," she greeted her friend, turning to look, and found — nobody there.

That was odd...first the unexplained voices, and now this. The fog was beginning to lift a little, and she could see that there was no way whatsoever that a living person could have walked up behind her like that and then simply vanished that quickly.

Apparently, she had company...of the spirit variety.

Cursing herself for not bringing a voice recorder, Emma pulled out her phone and began taking pictures, hoping to capture some visual evidence of this mysterious visitor. When she swiped through her camera reel, however, there was none to be found.

She waited for another ten minutes or so, slowly sipping her coffee. Whoever it had been was apparently not coming back, so Emma made her way across the road to the small cemetery she had seen when she had first arrived at the manor.

Snow began to fall. Stuffing her hands into the pockets of her jacket, Emma kept walking, slowly making her way from grave to grave.

And there it was again — the unmistakable sound of footsteps. They were following her, keeping perhaps ten or fifteen feet back. She stopped in her tracks and turn. The footsteps stopped too

Shaking her head, she resumed walking. So did the phantom footsteps. Emma's inner skeptic considered the possibility that they might be an echo of her own footsteps, but she was walking quietly on grass, not asphalt. The timing was also off, the sound of each footstep not syncing up with the impact of her soles on the ground.

Her ghostly companion was back.

Far from being a frightening experience, Emma actually found the fact that she was being followed by an unseen presence to be quite comforting.

As she walked from grave to grave, she paused to wipe away the light dusting of snow that obscured the name of the person buried there.

Finally, she found it: the headstone into which the words

'N.J. Franklin' were chiseled.

The grave that belonged to Nathan. His date of birth matched that which she had found in the records.

At the bottom of the faded gravestone was an inscription, difficult to read thanks to so many years of erosion and mold. Squatting down on her haunches, Emma brushed it clean. Its message was both simple and beautiful.

GONE, BUT NOT FORGOTTEN.

What a fine sentiment that was.

She reached out to touch the cold stone. She didn't know why Nathan had ended up living and working at the Poor Farm; nor did she know what it was that had taken his life at the age of 45. But standing there at his grave-side, she felt somehow connected to him, despite the decades and generations that separated them both. It was almost as if she could feel him standing there, keeping her silent company.

After reflecting on that for a while, she turned and headed back toward the manor. This time, the only footsteps to be heard were her own, leaving a single set of prints in the snow.

"I often think about Nathan," Emma told me, as she

recounted her strange experience on that cold and overcast morning. "I took everyone to the cemetery before we left. The feeling was peaceful, but it wasn't the same as the first time I had been there that morning.

"If I ever go back to the manor, I will be sure to have coffee with Nathan again. He may be gone, but he is not forgotten."

It is sad to think of just how many residents of the manor lived, died, and were buried there, only to go unremembered, the highs and the lows of their lives forever lost to the passage of time.

Emma's encounter with the paranormal may not be spectacular or terrifying, but it does raise an intriguing question: is it possible for somebody to form a connection with a spirit, purely through the act of focusing one's mental energy upon them?

In Emma's case, she selected a long-dead person at random, somebody who had lived and died at the location she was about to visit. By trying to learn as much as she possibly could about her chosen subject, Nathan, and his circumstances, did she somehow manage to forge a psychic link with him…one that resulted in his spirit coming to visit her early one misty morning?

While it is certainly possible that the footsteps which first approached Emma while she was sitting on the bench, and then followed her across to the old graveyard, belonged to one of the other resident spirits of the manor, it could also be the case that they were a manifestation of Nathan himself, paying a visit to the woman who had made sure that his earthly existence would never be forgotten.

CHAPTER ELEVEN
Wolf Man

Richelle is a 911 paramedic with an extensive background in fighting wildfires. She is an excellent medical provider, as I can attest from personal experience; we have worked together for many years, primarily on the medical side of things.

She also has the dubious honor of being a 'shit magnet,' the nickname that is bestowed on those medics who seem to attract the strangest, most difficult 911 calls. It sounds like a fun thing at first, until you realize that many of those calls tend to be fatality incidents, the sort that are capable of scarring you psychologically and emotionally.

Perhaps this is why Richelle is not a woman to mince words. She does not pull her punches when it comes to speaking out, and can be blunt almost to the point of tactlessness on occasion; this also means that she tells the truth, no matter what anybody else might think.

Coming from a Comanche background, Richelle grew up a spiritual person who had no trouble believing in the existence of a broader, larger world — one that contains ghosts, spirits, skinwalkers, and shapeshifters. It may seem strange for some people to believe that, in the twenty-first century, there are individuals roaming around out there that can change their form into that of an animal and back again (frankly, I have a hard time believing it myself) but to Richelle and those of a similar upbringing, this is simply a fact of life.

The wildfire came at a bad time, during the middle of a hot, dry fire season, the kind that the continental United States is beginning to see more and more frequently these days. Richelle was working as a specialized medical resource, or 'fireline medic,' which meant that she worked with the wildland firefighters in order to ensure their wellbeing and safety.

Wildland firefighting is an inherently risky and dangerous business. Tragedy is never more than an arm's reach away on larger incidents, when a shift in the weather can whip up a seemingly small, well-controlled fire into something terrifyingly unpredictable. Fire crews always maintain a healthy respect for the beast, usually working fourteen-day assignments on big fires, before taking a short break and heading on to the next.

For such crews, fighting wildland fire is a way of life, a vocation rather than being simply a job. They tend to be tight-knit, often to the point of becoming family. Bonds of loyalty run deep, particularly when a crew comes from the same locality, or, in the case of the crew that Richelle happened to be working with, the same Native American tribe.

Unlike Richelle, the fire crew were not Comanche; out of respect for them and in order to maintain their anonymity, I will not identify their tribal affiliation here. The lead medical unit leader remained at the command post back in fire camp, while Richelle was deployed closer to the fire itself.

Usually, crews such as this didn't talk a great deal to anybody who was outside their crew — unless, over the course of time, they got to know one another, and developed a degree of mutual trust.

Knowing Richelle as I do, it's fair to say that she pretty much steamrollered her way into their midst and *forced* them to engage with her. As someone with a similar cultural background, who was also heavily invested in their health and wellbeing, the crew didn't put up much of a fight. She has that kind of personality. It didn't take long for the crew to start trusting her, bringing her into the outer periphery of their circle.

One firefighter in particular really took a shine to her, and before long, he was confiding in her; he even began teaching her the language and dialect of their tribe. This was a huge compliment, not something to be taken lightly, and Richelle treated the gesture with the respect that it deserved.

The firefighter's nickname was 'Wolf Man.' This was not particularly unusual; many of those in the fire service have nicknames, usually relating to some defining physical characteristic or based upon something particularly memorable that they have done during their career. *Perhaps*, Richelle thought idly, *He's just a really hairy dude...*

"Alright," she asked, a few days later, when her curiosity had finally gotten the better of her. "I'll bite. Why do they cool you Wolf Man?"

Wolf Man smirked, saying nothing.

As the days stretched on, it became apparent that this was going to be a longer deployment than the standard two weeks; in fact, it would eventually run to twenty-one days.

Early one morning, the crew started out on the hike to the fireline. They hand-carried all of the tools, supplies, and equipment that they would need to work on the fire that day. Richelle went along with them, packing in all of the medical kit necessary to handle practically any emergency. She couldn't help but notice that the crew seemed to be in an odd mood that day. Something wasn't quite right with their demeanor, although she couldn't put her finger on precisely what it was.

The sun began to climb above the horizon as they walked toward the fireline, warming the air comfortably. By noon, it would become insufferably hot, and she was glad that her pack contained several bags of fluid and IV hook-ups in case anybody went down with heat stroke.

Before long, they had left all signs of even rural civilization behind. They were in the middle of nowhere, following the banks of a creek in order to maintain their sense of orientation. They approached a line of trees which demarcated the edge of a stretch of woodland.

Richelle was the first one to hear the drums, a rhythmic, staccato beat that was carried toward them on what little breeze there was. She recognized the type of melody. This was the sound of some sort of ceremony or ritual, and was coming from within the wood ahead of them.

What a strange thing to find out here. There are no homes for miles in any direction.

Suddenly, the drumming was accompanied by a chorus of singing and chanting. The crew passed into the shade of the trees, relieved to be out of the direct sunlight. Visibility was good, but Richelle couldn't see any sign of the mysterious drummers and singers; despite this, now that the firefighters had made it a few hundred feet into the woods, the sounds were coming from all around them.

After two more minutes, the chanting and drumming stopped. The firefighters stopped as well, shrugging off their packs and taking a five-minute break to drink a little water and rest their weary feet.

"Today's the day," one of them said, apropos of nothing. He unscrewed the cap from a water bottle and took a long swallow.

"Today's the day for *what?*" Richelle wanted to know.

"Good things are going to happen today," another said, cryptically. "Aren't they, Wolf Man?"

Wolf Man just smiled and looked away. Then he looked back at Richelle and said, "You'll see."

The crew worked hard until dusk, digging line, felling trees, and creating a fire break that would — hopefully — delay the spread of the wildfire. As the sun began to set in the west, they made the long hike back to base camp. During the walk, Richelle mulled over Wolf Man's words. *You'll see? You'll see **what?***

They took the same route back, passing through the woods, which were now a lot darker and gloomier than they had been earlier that morning. Once again, the sounds of chanting and drumming surrounded them, seeming to always be just a little way beyond the edge of sight.

"Do you guys hear that?" Richelle asked.

They seemed surprised that she was able to hear it too, and confirmed with her that the noise was the sound of some kind of tribal ceremony taking place.

"So, what is it?" The fire crew simply smiled at her in that infuriating way of theirs, as if they were privy to something that she didn't know yet.

Looking back with the benefit of hindsight, Richelle would come to realize that this was the exact moment at which they accepted her fully into their circle of trust.

It was a tired and footsore bunch of firefighters that marched into camp that evening. After debriefing the day's events, discussing the tactical plan for the next day, then grabbing some hot food and taking care of their personal hygiene, many of them decided to call it an early night. Richelle went into her tent, climbed into her sleeping bag, and soon fell fast asleep.

She awoke with a start three hours later. Night had

fallen, and Richelle lay there in the darkness, just listening. All was quiet in the camp, and she wondered just what it was that had caused her to wake up. *Something* wasn't quite right.

The sound of furtive movement came from just outside the tent. At first, she wondered if it was a fellow firefighter, lurking outside and getting ready to play a practical joke on her. Firefighters can be like that sometimes, though she would have been surprised if anybody had the energy left to do that after the strenuous day's work they had all just put in. Still, stranger things had happened.

The noise, whatever it was, began to recede. Sliding out of her sleeping bag, she made her way on all fours toward the tent opening and slowly slid the zipper on the window flap down. Richelle peered out into the darkness.

There, walking away from her tent and heading toward the treeline, was a huge wolf. The beast was a grayish-whitish color, and seemed quite content to be nosing around in the middle of a fire camp — something that regular wolves almost *never* did, unless they were starving or diseased.

How strange.

Still tired, Richelle climbed back into her sleeping bag

and went back to sleep.

At dawn the next morning, she and the crew met for breakfast.

"Man," one of the firefighters said between mouthfuls of food. "That was a *long* night last night."

There was a chorus of good-natured laughs, and all eyes turned toward Wolf Man.

"You must be tired, huh, Wolf Man?"

More laughs.

After yet another long and difficult day on the fireline, Richelle turned in early once more. Yet again, she was woken up a few hours later by the sounds of movement outside her tent. This time, when she looked outside, she saw Wolf Man, walking toward the edge of the woods. He was taking exactly the same path that the gray wolf had taken the night before.

She watched him disappear into the night, and couldn't help but wonder if this was coincidence...or something more.

On the thirteenth day of their deployment, Wolf Man approached Richelle. Sitting down next to her, he quietly asked what she knew about the tribe that he belonged to. After confessing her ignorance, he went on to explain that some of his people were able to shape-shift, changing their form into that of an animal and then back again.

"Some become an animal for the purposes of good," he said, looking her straight in the eye, "and some become an animal for evil."

"So how do you tell them apart?" Richelle asked.

"You don't." Wolf Man went on to tell her that he was capable of shape-shifting into a wolf. Instantly, the events of the past few days took on a new light in her mind. The nickname, Wolf Man; the joking references to it being an exhausting night; and the sight of the big wolf outside her tent, followed by the sighting of Wolf Man himself.

As crazy as it sounded, Richelle was convinced that he and the wolf were one and the same, heading to exactly the same place on those two consecutive nights.

Once Richelle had finished telling me this part of her story, I cleared my throat and asked her an awkward question.

"You're a medical professional. You have extensive training and education in the fields of emergency medicine, clinical pharmacology, anatomy, and physiology. You are also a clinical educator. I mean, you teach people about all aspects of the human body. So, I have to ask: how do you explain this notion of it being somehow able to change form into that of a wolf, or any other animal? It goes against pretty much every single law of physics that I've ever heard of."

She paused for a long moment, collecting her thoughts. Finally, she said, "I can't explain it. But I believe it. I just can't tell you how it happens, but it *does.*"

Over the course of the next few nights, Wolf Man would disappear into the woods, making no attempt to hide his movements. Then would come the sound of a wolf — sometimes, multiple wolves — howling and baying in the darkness.

"Can other members of your crew do the same thing?" Richelle asked. Wolf Man failed to reply, answering only with a knowing smile and a wink.

She had noticed that, despite the sense of humor they all shared, the fire crew treated Wolf Man with a great deal of respect and deference, even those members who were tribal elders. She came to suspect that this was because of his extraordinary ability to shift form.

"Wolf Man told you that some shape-shifters use their abilities for good, and others for evil," I probed. "Which do you think he was?"

Richelle didn't hesitate. "To be perfectly honest, he had

a little bit of a dark side to him. But people are complex, shades of gray. I think he was able to control those darker aspects of his nature."

One day, late in the deployment, the crew chanced upon what looked to be an old, abandoned house in the middle of the wilderness. A deer skull had been placed rather deliberately on the wooden steps leading up to the front door. Directly above the door, a dead crow had been spread out, its outstretched wings nailed to the frame.

The message was clear: **keep out.**

The fire crew wanted no part of going inside. Something ritualistic — something dark — had taken place here. Everybody sensed it. These were evil omens, they believed, and Richelle was inclined to agree with them. Wolf Man simply smiled, hopped over the skull, ducked underneath the decomposing crow, and pushed his way through the front door without an apparent care in the world.

"Richelle, you go in too!" they urged. "Follow him inside!"

It was the last thing in the world she wanted to do, but having worked so hard to earn their trust and respect, Richelle didn't want to lose face with them right now. She may never get it back. Taking a deep breath, she picked her way gingerly across the deer skull, trying her best to ignore the hollow eye sockets which stared blindly up at her. Duckwalking beneath the body of the crow, she made her way into the entranceway.

This was a nice house (if a little bit isolated) and one that ought to be worth a lot of money...so why had it been abandoned? There hadn't been any mandatory evacuations in the area due to the fire.

The atmosphere hit her like a heavy weight landing on her head. It felt tense and oppressive. Richelle's heart began to race from the moment she first set foot in the hallway. Something very, very bad had taken place here. As she went carefully from room to room, she noticed that there was nothing in the way of personal effects — family photographs, mementos — to be seen. It looked sterile and antiseptic, as if nobody had lived here for a long, long time.

In the living room, the sun-bleached skull of a small animal had been placed front and center, surrounded by bird feathers in a ritualistic manner. Richelle shied away from it, her sense of deep unease growing, but Wolf Man gave the occult array a look of great interest, as though admiring the handiwork of a fellow practitioner.

For the remainder of the day, the mood among the crew

was a little more subdued than usual.

At the end of the deployment, Richelle and the crew went their separate ways, and although they kept in touch sporadically, ever since that day, she has looked at wolves in an entirely different light.

CHAPTER TWELVE

Dead Man Walking

Post-Traumatic Stress Disorder (PTSD) is, sadly, an all too common consequence for those who work in the emergency services. This should come as no great surprise to anybody, considering the awful things that we are called to deal with on a daily basis.

Almost every police officer, firefighter, EMT, or paramedic has that call — that one call — which haunts them, sometimes for years or even decades afterward. It doesn't necessarily have to be particularly gruesome; anything that can strike a personal chord is often enough to imprint it on you forever.

My own personal example came when I was working as a firefighter-paramedic one evening. We had just started our shift, when we were dispatched to a 'code black.' This is emergency-speak for an obvious death, and usually means that there are signs of rigor mortis, decomposition, decapitation, or some form of unsurvivable traumatic injury.

Stephanie, the other paramedic working with me that night, was also driving the fire truck. As we pulled up outside a small house, she asked me if I wanted her to go and take care of the pronouncement.

"That's okay, Steph. You're driving tonight, and I haven't done anything useful yet. I'll take this one."

She didn't take much convincing. I'd be the one to write the report and file the paperwork afterward, something that nobody really enjoys doing. As I was getting down from the fire engine, a police officer came walking up to me. We fell into step together, heading for the back door.

"Looks like he's been dead for a while," the officer said. "Hasn't been seen for a week. The guy who cuts the grass saw him through the window and called 911."

It was late evening, and dark inside the house when I stuck my head around the back door, which opened directly onto the kitchen. In the gloom, I could just make out a figure hunched in the middle of the floor. Switching on my flashlight, I could see that it was the body of an older gentlemen; although it was tough to tell, I estimated him to be in his late sixties or early seventies.

The man's skin had the sallow, waxen look of the dead. He was curled up in the fetal position, knees drawn up into his chest. His mouth was open, and a pool of dark, sticky blood had dripped from it, spreading around the side of his head. All of the blood had drained toward the ground, leaving the bottom part of his body a deep purple color.

This was going to be a simple call, what we sometimes refer to as a 'doorway pronouncement' — in other words, the signs of death were so apparent that I didn't need to go any further than the doorway to confirm the fact that he was beyond any possibility of resuscitation. My best guess was that he had been walking across the kitchen, perhaps getting himself something to eat or drink, and had dropped dead very suddenly. The chances were that it had been a quick death, and one without much in the way of pain or fear.

I called the hospital, spoke to a physician, and obtained an official time of death. That was all that I needed to do in order to make this a legal pronouncement of death. Then I left the scene in the hands of the police, who would determine whether any sort of investigation was warranted, before they turned it over to the coroner.

Ten minutes later, I was back at the fire house, eating dinner and shooting the breeze with my crew. I didn't think too much about our field pronouncement for the rest of the evening. We ran a couple of calls, and then went to bed at around midnight.

I woke up at two o'clock, needing to use the toilet. I stepped out of my bunk room into the hallway outside.

There, at the end of the darkened corridor, was my patient. He was just standing there, outside the captain's bedroom, staring back at me. He looked exactly as he had a few hours ago, except this time, his eyes were open and staring.

Blinking, he was gone. I told myself that my mind was playing tricks, went to the restroom, and crawled back into bed. For the rest of the night, in between 911 calls, I had a series of very similar nightmares in which I saw the dead man walking around the fire station, opening up doors at random. I woke in a cold sweat after each one, my heart pounding in my chest.

This happened for a couple of nights at home, too. As a paranormal investigator and writer of books such as the one you are now reading, you might think I would jump to the conclusion that the spirit of the dead man had followed me back to the fire station, and then home. But that wasn't it at all.

You see, when I was a teenager, I was the one to discover the dead body of my grandfather. He died very quickly, walking from his living room into the kitchen. His body was curled up in the fetal position on the carpet, knees to chest, just as the patient had been. It was the first corpse I had ever seen, and as a relatively young lad, it had spooked me more than a little, especially because it was the body of a man that I loved and idolized. I carry that mental image around with me to this day.

The position of the deceased patient had triggered something in my brain, that familiar memory of my grandfather's death, and it had begun to wreak havoc on my subconscious mind while I was sleeping. The only ghost involved here was a ghost from my childhood, a deeply-unpleasant memory coming to the fore because of the similarity between the positioning of the two bodies.

I do not, to the very best of my knowledge, have PTSD. The nightmares soon stopped and life went back to normal. Not every first responder is so fortunate. Many of them live with the consequences of post-traumatic stress on a daily basis.

Richelle does have PTSD, and is all too aware of the fact. This awareness means that she is able to recognize her signs and symptoms when they occur. Sometimes her brain plays tricks on her, but she is not given to seeing things that are not there. That is an important thing to bear in mind when it comes to the story that follows.

The crash was a bad one, on a road that was well-known for bad wrecks. The motorcycle had been going fast, well above the speed limit, when it had wiped out; its rider had been ejected from the bike and thrown through the air. Despite the helmet he wore, he had sustained a major head injury on impact, along with a multitude of other broken bones.

Richelle's ambulance was the second-arriving unit. A fire engine was already on-scene, its crew doing their best to save the injured man's life. As she walked up to the site of the crash, medical kit bag slung over one shoulder, it became very apparent that things did not look good.

The motorcyclist had broken several ribs and ruptured a lung. His clothes had been cut away, revealing the fact that one side of his chest was barely expanding in comparison to the other. Kneeling down in the wet grass at the side of the road, Richelle removed a large needle and inserted it into a space beneath his armpit, just above the fifth rib.

When the tip of the needle punctured the muscle and connective tissue, working its way into the chest cavity, a hiss of pressurized air was accompanied by a spurt of blood. Now that she had evacuated the pressure on the lung, his chances of survival had improved slightly.

The EMS crew worked efficiently and methodically,

securing the airway with a plastic tube, taking over breathing for the patient, and then, as they headed off to the hospital with lights flashing and sirens blaring, starting an IV in each arm.

Despite their very best efforts, the man died later at the hospital.

It was a difficult call to run, both technically and emotionally. What was worse, Richelle's house overlooked the street on which it had happened. She had her own way of coping with bad days like this — she liked to ride her motorcycle, feeling the wind in her hair and allowing her mind to go blank, free of all cares and worries.

On the day of the man's funeral, Richelle hopped on the bike and took off. She rode around the streets of the city, without any particular destination in mind. This was all about the journey, the process of cleansing her mind of negative energies.

As she crested the rise of a fairly steep hill, about a mile away from the scene of the accident, Richelle came to a four-way intersection. Looking from left to right in order to clear traffic, she suddenly did a double-take. When she took a left turn, there, standing on the opposite side of the road not ten feet away from her, was the dead man.

He was wearing the same clothes he had worn on the night of the crash. The low speed limit at the intersection meant she had plenty of time to blink, to check that what she was seeing was something that she really WAS seeing. He didn't disappear, but rather, slowly turned his head to watch her as she rode past. His eyes locked on to hers for a moment. She saw no judgment there, no accusation; no hint of, "Why couldn't you save me?" or "Why didn't you try harder?"

She felt no guilt after the call. Everything had gone as well as anybody could have expected. Some injuries are just too severe to be fixable. The fire and EMS crew had performed to the highest professional standard, but the severity of trauma was too great.

The man gave the slightest nod of acknowledgment, and then she was past him. Turning to look over her shoulder, Richelle fully expected him to have disappeared, but lo and behold, there he was, lingering on the street corner and watching her ride away.

Meanwhile, at that very same time, his body was being committed to the ground several miles away.

Due to her PTSD, Richelle has a tendency to re-live the calls that bother her, replaying the events over and over again in her mind, as if she was right back there on-scene. The victims also had the same injuries that they had sustained during the actual incident.

What she didn't see, was the deceased victims hanging out on street corners. That just wasn't the way that her symptoms manifested. She was convinced that each sighting of the dead man was neither a figment of her imagination, nor a side-effect of the call's traumatic nature.

She was seeing him, as clear as day.

Richelle turned to a trusted Native American spiritual teacher for advice. Why, she wanted to know, had the dead man been there, at exactly the right time for her to encounter him?

Perhaps, her teacher opined, this was his way of indicating his approval; a short visit from the afterlife, in order to make her aware that she had done the very best she could, and that everything was going to be okay.

The more she thought about it, the more Richelle liked that explanation. The dead man has never appeared to her again. Presumably, his work now done, he has now moved on into the great unknown that awaits us all on the other side of death.

CHAPTER THIRTEEN
Dark Passenger

Danny currently serves as a Border Force (customs) officer in the United Kingdom. In a former career, however, he worked in the field of psychiatric care, primarily on secure units in mental health hospitals and prisons.

One such facility was an all-male institution that housed over 200 patients, many of them highly dangerous; almost all have been convicted of committing extremely violent crimes, or in some cases, found to be mentally incompetent to stand trial for those crimes, by reason of insanity.

The facility began life as a criminal lunatic asylum during the 1800s, and as such, had more than sufficient reason to be haunted; one can only imagine the long-tern effect of years of pent-up emotional energy within those walls.

Danny worked on a ward that housed female patients, four of whom were deemed to be of such a risk that they were kept in total isolation, allowed out only in complete restraints. These were greatly disturbed individuals. Teams of carers were assigned to go into their cells in order to clean and feed them.

Late one night, Danny was walking along one of the corridors on the female wing, heading for the kitchen. In order to get there, he had to pass through several heavy locked doors, which made for something of an inconvenience, but was an absolutely critical safety measure when it came down to keeping the inmates securely contained.

The corridor and the small dining room were in complete darkness. Danny walked into the kitchen, switched on the lights, and began to collect mugs and cups in preparation for making some tea.

Sudden movement behind him caused Danny to whirl around. There, standing in the doorway through which he had just passed, was a black figure. For a split-second, he thought it was a patient, but it soon became all too apparent that this wasn't a human being at all. While it was human shaped, the dark thing had no features whatsoever.

It bolted toward him. Danny braced for impact. He had seen far too many colleagues assaulted by patients at the facility, and so his reflexes instantly kicked in, causing him to bring up the tray of cups he was carrying in front of his body as a form of shield, spilling hot tea and coffee over himself in the process.

But there was no impact. The figure simply disappeared, leaving him standing all alone in the middle of a pool of hot liquid.

Danny's heart was racing. What on Earth had just happened? He wracked his brains trying to find a logical explanation for it. Nobody had been in the kitchen or dining room when he had come in, of that he was completely sure. That left the darkened hallway outside through which he had come. Perhaps, he thought dubiously, somebody had been lurking out there in the shadows, waiting for him to come in. He dismissed the notion immediately as being ridiculous; for starters, nobody — whether escaped prisoner or staff member — *looked* like that, or had the ability to disappear into thin air while still in plain sight, for that matter.

Nonetheless, he retraced his steps out into the corridor and confirmed that the steel door was indeed still closed securely and locked up tight. There it was, just as he had left it when he came through to make the drinks.

He was all alone, and had just been rushed by a shadow figure. There was no way he was ever going to admit what had just happened to his colleagues.

"These facilities have an aura," Danny reflects, "and they hold on to some of the pain and negative emotion from the people who spent years there. I think that what attacked me was the *shell* of somebody that had been a patient or inmate at the secure hospital in the past."

Nor was it the only inexplicable incident that happened to him during his tenure there.

One part of the campus was an occupational therapy (OT) section, where female inmates would go during the day to paint and spend time engaged in arts and crafts, as part of the ongoing efforts to rehabilitate them. The OT department was not used at night, which made it all the stranger when at around three o'clock one morning, Danny saw a warning light flashing. It signified a problem in the OT wing.

Security officers immediately responded. Cautiously, they made entry into the building, switching on the lights as they went. Although there were no signs of forcible entry, one of the manual alarm buttons had been pushed. Somebody would have needed to be standing directly in front of it in order to set the alarm off, yet the OT building was securely locked and none of the motion sensors had been set off.

This wasn't the first time such an incident had taken place. Electricians had been called in to check out the alarm system, and declared everything to be working normally. It's worth noting that this was the oldest part of the hospital. The nocturnal operation of the facility was overseen by a night manager, who liked nothing more than to creep onto the wards after dark in an attempt to catch the staff members sleeping. One night, Danny and a colleague were engaged in an observational session, which entailed spending two hours sitting and watching the rooms and corridors to make sure that all was well.

Suddenly, they heard the sound of keys rattling. Both of them pricked up their ears. The noise had come from the end of the hallway that the night manager would use to make entry into the female wing of the hospital.

"Here he comes," Danny whispered to his colleague. "Sit up straight and look alert." Neither of them had been sleeping, but it made sense to make a good impression in front of the boss.

Then came the sound of something rustling, followed by that of footsteps coming toward them along the hallway. They stopped about halfway down. Danny's colleague stood up and went to see who was prowling around in the wee small hours of the morning.

"You're not going to believe this, Danny, but there's nobody there…"

Both of them were thinking the same thing. This particular wing of the hospital was said to be haunted by a gray lady, the ghost of a former matron. The stories claimed that her manifestation was usually accompanied by the sound of her starched uniform rustling as she walked along, checking each cell to make sure that everything was in order.

Many staff members reported hearing the rustling, and the sound of doors being unlocked — always at night, and always on the female wards. Whenever they went to check, the patients were always securely locked in their cells, and nobody was ever found walking the corridors.

This cyclical pattern of behavior bears all the hallmarks of a residual-type haunting. In other words, this may not be an intelligent, interactive spirit at all, but rather, a form of paranormal recording, made when the gray lady was a living, breathing person. As she made her rounds each night, walking the same route over and over again, elements of this activity (primarily the audible ones) were somehow imprinted on the environment, and could then be 'played back' many years later when circumstances were right. Talk to the night staff at any of the older, historic hospitals, and it's a safe bet that you will hear similar stories. Gray ladies, in particular, seem to be especially common, perhaps because gray was once a very common color of nursing uniform.

Sometimes, the otherwise-peaceful nights at the secure hospital were broken by the sound of screaming. On one particular night, Danny and a colleague were startled to hear a woman shrieking, coming from somewhere inside the hospital wing next to theirs. From the sound of it, all hell was breaking loose. They immediately broke into a run, bursting onto the neighboring ward and all set to help contain whatever emergency was taking place...only to have their colleagues meet them with a very strange look on their faces.

No, they said, there was no emergency. All of the inmates were safely tucked up in their beds, with the cell doors locked. Nobody had heard any screaming. Were Danny and his colleagues sure that they hadn't simply imagined it...?

On another night shift, no less than *five* people on Danny's team witnessed the sight of the door handle on the community washroom being violently jiggled, as if somebody was trapped inside and was trying desperately to get out. The washroom was empty and locked.

A number of the nurses had come from Jamaica and

Mauritius, and shared with Danny stories of the ghostly goings-on in their own hospitals back home. He soon learned that the phenomenon of the haunted hospital was one that seemed to cross all cultural and geographical boundaries.

There is an old superstition among emergency responders and medical professionals that the full moon brings an increase in the level of strange and bizarre activity that we are asked to deal with. While there is very little scientific evidence to back that up, anecdotally speaking, most of us will tell you that it is nonetheless true.

The secure hospital was home to a number of patients who were held in conditions of long-term isolation, as much for their own protection as that of everybody else. For those poor unfortunate souls who were so mentally and emotionally disturbed that there was simply no possibility of a cure, this would be their home for the rest of their natural lives.

One such lady was placed under Danny's care. She liked to speak to herself, which wasn't at all unusual on the ward, but Danny's interest was piqued one night when he very clearly heard a voice answering her...a *male* voice. The man sounded as if he was in deep conversation with the female patient.

As he walked toward her cell, Danny could see her through the observation slit in the steel door. She was kneeling down, lit only by the moonlight that came through the cell's single window.

"Who are you talking to you?" Danny asked, without unlocking the door and going into the room. This had never happened before.

She turned toward him, and without speaking another word, offered him a grin that didn't look as if it belonged on her face at all. Perhaps it was just the way the moonlight caught her features, Danny told himself, but it really did appear as if somebody else was looking back at him from behind the woman's eyes...

I encountered a similar situation when I investigated a haunted residential care facility in Iowa, known as Malvern Manor. One of the better-known residents was a lady named Gracie, who had been diagnosed with multiple personality disorder. The care staff and nurses regularly heard the sound of many different voices coming from inside Gracie's room, a number of them male. One particularly gruff and angry voice would repeat the phrase, "The Devil's coming to get me," over and over again. Whenever anybody went in to check, Gracie was always alone — the voices all came from inside her.

What's fascinating about this, from a paranormal investigator's point of view, is that visitors to Malvern Manor today still report hearing the sound of those voices coming from inside the walls of Gracie's room. This begs the question: do multiple personalities somehow take on a life of their own, and can they independently survive bodily death — or is this a purely residual auditory phenomenon, like that of the gray lady encountered by Danny and his colleague?

For his part, Danny wonders just how many supposedly schizophrenic patients are actually playing host to some kind of 'dark passenger.' It is a phenomenon he saw many times during his career in the field of mental health. Could some of them actually be possessed, rather than mentally ill?

It certainly makes you think.

CHAPTER FOURTEEN
The Boy

Richard works as a paramedic in a busy part of the British 999 ambulance system, which covers four counties and serves hundreds of thousands of people. In addition to that, he works in the area of community access, teaching members of the public how to use defibrillators. Having worked in the field of emergency medicine for more than twenty years, there really isn't a lot that he hasn't seen…or so he thought.

His personal brush with the paranormal took place back in the mid-1990s. Richard and his partner were dispatched to what was known as a 'blue call,' which meant that while their ambulance was not directed to respond with lights flashing and sirens wailing, it was nonetheless considered to be an emergency, and therefore a high priority.

A physician had made a house call on an elderly lady, and after assessing her carefully, had deemed her condition to be serious enough to require that she be admitted to the hospital. When they heard this news, the responding EMS crew understood why they had been asked to respond. Had things been a little more serious, then they would have been running on a 'red' call, driving under emergency rules.

While his partner drove, Richard helped him by navigating. When he looked up the address on the map, he saw that it was located in a small village that was a fair distance away from the nearest hospital.

It was coming to the end of the day, one of those warm summer days which make living in the English countryside such a delight. The sun was setting, but there was plenty of daylight left. The ambulance turned off the side road onto a gravel driveway, one which led to a rustic-looking thatched cottage.

Once the parking brake had been set, Richard and his partner got out of the ambulance and went around to the back of the vehicle to remove the wheeled stretcher. Their cardiac monitor and medical kit bag were sitting on top of the bed. As the two medics pushed the stretcher along, the front door of the cottage opened. A middle-aged lady and her young daughter emerged.

"We're so glad you're here," she said, offering them a smile that seemed fraught with worry. "Mum's feeling a little poorly, and the doctor thinks that she needs to go in to be looked at."

Assuring her that it was no problem at all, Richard

followed the lady inside, leaving the stretcher at the front door and slinging the medical kit bag over his shoulder. His partner grabbed the carry chair, figuring that the fairly narrow hallway would be a nightmare to maneuver the stretcher through...at least, not without scraping the wallpaper off on either side, something that would be very poor form.

One of the back rooms had been turned into a long-term bedroom. The medics found their patient sitting up in bed, fully conscious and coherent. While his partner took a knee and started chatting with the patient (and beginning his own physical assessment at the same time) Richard went back to the ambulance. Knowing that they were going to use the carry chair rather than the stretcher, it seemed like a good idea to back the ambulance a little closer to the cottage. That way, there would be less likelihood of one of them tripping on the gravel pathway and dumping their precious cargo.

After loading the unused stretcher back up, Richard turned back toward the cottage...and stopped. There, standing in the doorway, was a young boy with black hair. He simply stood there, holding onto the frame with one hand, gazing calmly back at the paramedic. There was something slightly...*off* about him, and it took Richard a second to figure out what it was. The boy's clothing looked a little out of place, or perhaps more accurately, out of *time*. The red sweater and bell-bottomed blue jeans would have been more at home in the 1970s than the 1990s.

And then he was gone, ducking back inside the house.

Richard shrugged and followed him inside, thinking nothing more of it. He simply assumed that the lady of the house had another child, a son, along with the daughter that he had already met.

Making his way to back to the bedroom once again, he found the old lady sitting up on the edge of her bed, ready to go. The medics helped her across to the carry chair, buckled her in securely with seat belts, and maneuvered her carefully out of the house. They made it without putting a single scratch on either the walls or the furniture.

The mother and daughter followed them out. Once their patient was loaded up in the back of the ambulance and in the care of his partner, Richard turned to speak with her daughter, who said that she and her own daughter would be following behind the ambulance in their car.

"Don't forget your son," the paramedic said with a smile, just as she began to swing the door shut.

"Son?" The lady seemed confused. "I…don't have a

son."

Richard described the black-haired young boy that he had seen standing in the cottage doorway. "I saw him as clear as day, just as clearly as I'm seeing you standing in front of me right now."

More to humor him than anything else, the lady made a show of going back inside and searching the cottage room by room.

It was completely empty.

Now it was Richard's turn to be confused. "I don't understand…I *saw* him…I know I did."

He was convinced that the young lad had not been a product of his imagination, some kind of visual hallucination brought on by fatigue or overwork. He had been as solid as any flesh and blood person, with just the slightest hint of unreality about him.

But if that was so, where had he gone? There was no way he could have gotten past Richard after he had ducked back inside the cottage, and there had been no sign of him inside the house.

That could only mean one thing.

Richard had just seen a ghost.

Despite what you may have seen on TV, the majority of ghost sightings are not dark, terrifying, and spectacular. In fact, most of them are very similar to Richard's experience. Quite often, the eyewitness doesn't realize that what they are actually seeing is an apparition until after the encounter has ended.

That was certainly true of my own brush with an apparition. It happened on Halloween night (I know, I know!) at the old Tooele Valley Hospital, located in the city of Tooele, Utah. The hospital is now a full-contact Halloween haunted house named Asylum 49, and also happens to be one of the most haunted locations I have ever come across. (Asylum 49 is covered in the next chapter).

The owners were kind enough to let myself and a team of fellow paranormal researchers investigate the hospital over the course of several nights. We picked the week of Halloween deliberately, mostly because that is when the paranormal activity is said to be at its peak.

But first, we had to wait for the haunt to be over and for the customers to leave — hundreds of terrified people being chased by chainsaw-wielding demonic doctors and nurses are not exactly conducive to carrying out a successful paranormal investigation, after all.

Never one to sit around and twiddle my thumbs, I decided to go through the haunt myself, experiencing it from the inside just as the customers did. Even though I knew where each monster was, I still got caught out several times by a jump scare, and my heart skipped more than a few beats as I made my way along those haunted hallways, moving from room to room and scare to scare.

After running across a particularly creepy mutant *something*, I came up on a crossroads, where several corridors branched off in a number of different directions. I picked one at random, and had gone no more than a few feet when I saw a young girl frightening the life out of a lady in her twenties. The girl couldn't have been much older than seven or eight at the very most. She was garbed like Goldilocks, in an old-style dress, and had long hair. She was gripping the woman's forearm and tugging on it, trying to drag her into a side room — and pretty much succeeding.

For her part, the woman wore an expression that seemed to say, "Okay kid, I'll play along, but I *really* don't want to go in there." As I watched, the girl pulled her inside, and the door closed behind them both.

Much like Richard during his sighting of the dark-haired boy, I thought nothing more of it until I got to the end of the haunt and joined the owners of Asylum 49 in the control room.

"How was it?" they asked.

"Great fun!" I enthused, before adding, "I'm surprised that you let kids as young as that little girl work in the haunt though. I would have thought that an adult could accidentally hurt one of them if they were to panic."

"What girl?" they asked.

"You know, the Goldilocks girl," I said, the smile freezing on my face as reality began to sink in. I described her location exactly. They consulted the staffing plan, and said that no young actress had been assigned to that particular room, or anywhere even close to it. "But I saw her. She was completely solid!"

Even though the haunt had closed down for the night, none of the cast members had left yet. They were milling around in the break room, getting out of costume, having their make-up removed, and enjoying a soft drink and a snack as they chatted with one another about the thrills and chills of the night. Along with the owners, I looked at each and every one of them. The little girl I had seen so very clearly was not a member of the cast. I would stake my life upon it.

Our next stop was the front gate, where ticket sales took place. The gate agents assured us that they had let no children through that night who met that description.

So, who could the little girl have been? Unlike in Richard's case, we soon came up with the answer. The old hospital was said to be haunted by the spirits of two young girls who died there many years ago. According to the eyewitnesses who have encountered these apparitions, one of them bears an almost uncanny resemblance to the girl I saw in the hallway.

For years now, I have asked the question why, in an age in which practically *everybody* has a camera in their pocket (thanks to the miracle of cell phone technology) we do not have many truly impressive photographs of apparitions. Time after time, witnesses have told me that they never thought to pull out their phone and snap a picture because it never occurred to them that what they were looking at might be a ghost.

I found that a little difficult to understand, right up until that fateful Halloween night. It never crossed my mind that the young girl could be a spirit entity. She did not, for even a moment, seem like anything other than a perfectly ordinary flesh-and-blood child, one who was just having a lot of fun in a haunted house attraction.

If only I had known…

CHAPTER FIFTEEN

Asylum

Most paranormal investigators have a favorite haunted location, those places we feel a strong affinity with. They draw us back, over and over again, exerting some strange compulsion that can be difficult to understand, let alone explain to others.

For me, that place is the old Tooele Valley Hospital, or as it is now more commonly known...Asylum 49.

I first heard of the place back in 2015, when I was conducting research for the book that would become *The World's Most Haunted Hospitals*. It certainly had an intriguing back-story. After serving the Utah community of Tooele (including the nearby army depot) for several decades, the hospital had been supplanted by a newer, more modern facility. Many of the employees left in order to go and work at the new hospital, and as staffing levels dwindled, the Tooele Valley Hospital entered a downward spiral from which it would never escape.

When the death knell finally sounded, it happened quickly. The last patients were transferred out. The doctors, nurses, technicians, and janitors went home for the last time.

Then, the doors were locked, the hospital was closed up, and the sprawling facility that had served the people of Tooele faithfully for so many years, was left to fall apart.

Things might not have turned out for the best had it not been for a man by the name of Kimm Anderson. Kimm was well-versed in the haunted house scene — that is, the type of monster-filled attractions that seem to pop up everywhere in the weeks before Halloween. Visiting the abandoned old hospital one day, he immediately recognized its potential for becoming something unique: a medically-themed haunted house.

Along with members of his family, Kimm soon took ownership of the hospital. On first setting foot inside, he had expected to find the place stripped bare of all its fixtures and fittings; in fact, nothing could have been further from the truth.

It looked, to all intents and purposes, as if the hospital staff had simply walked out at the end of their last working day and left everything behind them. Beds, wheelchairs, medical supplies...even a fully-functioning X-ray machine were all left behind. Sharps containers full of needles remained bolted to the walls in the emergency room, never emptied of their bio-hazardous contents.

As Kimm walked around the place, moving from room to room, the only sound was the echoing of his own footsteps. He could already see, in his mind's eye, what the hospital would like when it was full of mask-wearing monsters and ghouls, leaping out of the darkness to scare the living daylights out of visiting customers.

There was only one catch…

…this haunted house really *was* haunted.

He first realized this when he felt an unseen hand tugging firmly at his leg. Over the years that followed, Kimm and his family took the Asylum 49 attraction from strength to strength, recruiting talented local youths and adult volunteers, and forming them into a close-knit family that is still going strong some ten years later.

They consider the spirits of the hospital to be an important part of that family.

Kimm and his wife, Cami, invited me to visit the hospital as part of the research for my book. I made the long road trip from Colorado on a sunny spring day, and spent a night prowling the hallways, conducting an eight-hour paranormal investigation session with two colleagues. The end result: nothing.

"The problem is that you came at the wrong time of

year," the Andersens explained to me afterward. "We were doing some construction, which can sometimes stir the spirits up a little bit, but they don't get really active until Halloween comes around."

The more I thought about it, the more that made sense to me. Thousands of people pass through the doors of Asylum 49 each and every Halloween season. It has a fearsome reputation, and one that is richly deserved. Because of the fact that it is a full contact haunt (visitors have to sign waivers, consenting to being touched, pushed, and physically manhandled) people come from far and wide to experience it for themselves.

Every single one of those people turned up at the Asylum 49 ticket booth with one single goal in mind: to get scared, albeit with the understanding that they would be completely safe. When you consider the sheer amount of fear that would permeate the old hospital on its busiest nights — not to mention the adrenaline-fueled excitement and glee of the cast members, who really throw themselves into their work — you have what is essentially, to quote *Ghost Adventures'* host Zak Bagans, a ghost factory. It has long been theorized that emotional energy can fuel paranormal activity. If that is indeed the case (I have certainly come to believe it to be true) then it is no wonder that during the month of October, the former Tooele Valley Hospital becomes one of the most paranormally active places in the country...if not the world.

"I'd love to come back," I told the Andersens, "but it's a long drive for just a day or two."

"Come for a week," they offered. Which is how I found myself, along with a small team of trusted paranormal investigators, taking up residence in the hospital that following Halloween.

To say that it was an eventful week would be a huge understatement. Readers who would like to learn more about what took place can read about it in detail within the pages of *The Haunting of Asylum 49*, written by myself and co-author Cami Andersen.

For three years, I went back there each Halloween, pitching in to help out with the haunt during opening hours, and then investigating the paranormal activity after midnight, when the last customer had left the building. One of the most interesting things about the whole situation was that only half of the sprawling hospital building was used as part of the haunt attraction. On the opposite side of the structure was a residential nursing facility, in which senior citizens and those with special needs were cared for around the clock.

A long central hallway ran from one end of the hospital to the other. Thanks to the green carpet that covered it, this stretch of corridor had been nicknamed the 'Green Mile,' after the popular Stephen King book and movie of the same name. For those entire three years, neither I nor any member of my team was ever allowed to cross the threshold from the Asylum 49 side to the nursing home side. Access was prevented by two very sturdy wooden doors that were situated at the far end of the Green Mile. They were kept securely locked at all times, and I completely understood why. It would hardly be decent to expose the elderly residents to the blood-curdling screams, shrieks, and antics that went on during the haunt; nor would they want people like me wandering around with digital recorders, attempting to capture EVPs. They deserved peace, quiet, and above all else, a little privacy.

Nevertheless, I found the idea of the nursing home intriguing. Perhaps this was partly because it was off-limits to us — forbidden fruit, so to speak — but I had also seen the episode of *Ghost Adventures* in which the stars of the show came to Asylum 49. They wandered across to the nursing home side, and somehow managed to get the employees to show them around. (I suspect that this unlooked-for publicity was not welcomed by the owners of the facility, and understandably so).

The nursing staff told disturbing stories of an ominous, ghostly man in black, who seemed to act like a harbinger of death — whenever this mysterious apparition was seen going into a patient's room, they would invariably die soon afterwards.

Psychic mediums had made the claim that the Green Mile was protected by a custodian: the spirit of a nurse named Maria, whose purpose was to act as a gatekeeper of sorts. It was said that whenever somebody passed away on the occupied side of the building, Maria made sure that they went to where they were supposed to go… and kept them away from the Asylum 49 side of things.

For years, I simply assumed that I would never get the chance to investigate the locked side of the building…but all that changed in January 2017, when the owners of the haunt finally realized their long-standing dream. The nursing home patients were being moved to a newer facility off-site, and the owners were willing to sell their portion of the building.

In short, the entirety of the old hospital would now

belong to Asylum 49…and I would be privileged to lead the first paranormal investigation by an outside team.

It was a paranormal investigator's dream come true, and I could hardly believe my good fortune. Along with a handful of trusted fellow investigator, I caught a flight to Salt Lake City and drove to Tooele, where Cami and Kimm Andersen met me at the front door, along with fellow owner Dusty Kingston.

"Come on in!" Cami grinned, after greeting us all with a hug. Cami is half my height and weighs about as much as my right leg, and this little tornado of energy is also an incredible paranormal investigator. She has also spent countless hours prowling the hallways of Asylum 49, doing her own research and looking for answers to the plethora of unexplained phenomena that are reported there.

We could have asked for no better guide to accompany us on our latest adventure. Cami led the way through the bowels of the old hospital. As we passed through now-familiar places such as the gift shop, our sense of excitement heightened. By the time we reached the double doors leading to the Green Mile, my hands were practically shaking with anticipation.

I turned the corner and found that those doors were not

only unlocked, but were also, for the first time, standing wide open. They seemed to be almost beckoning us to go through.

"Look up," Cami said, pointing at a CCTV security camera mounted directly above the doors. Nothing unusual about that, you might think, but when the new owners had first taken possession of the building, they had found a strip of tape across the lens. Curious as to why, they had spoken with a former employee, who told them that when the night staff would sit at the nurses' station, they would constantly see shadowy human-shaped figures walking back and forth in front of those doors. Finally, to prevent them from getting any more spooked than they already were, somebody had deliberately blacked out the camera.

Exactly how frightened of what they were seeing on that screen must they have been, in order to do something like that? I found myself asking, while also reminding myself that this was anecdotal evidence only, and should therefore be treated with due caution.

For the first time ever, I walked the entire length of the Green Mile, passing rooms I hadn't know existed. To my left was the old surgical suite, where thousands of operations had once taken place. Peering inside, I saw that some of the original equipment and fixtures was still there.

The long hallway climbed steeply, finally terminating at a T-junction. To the right were a number of residential rooms, all now empty. To the left was the nurse's station. Cami was kind enough to explain the layout of the place. It was a spoke-and-hub design: the nurse's station and its surrounding common area was the hub, the central nexus, and from there, several long hallways branched off as spokes. Each one of those wings had its own specialized purpose. For example, one ward was devoted to memory care — patients afflicted with dementia — and another took care of those who were in the end stages of their lives.

Taking my leave of Cami and my fellow investigators, I wandered off on my own for a bit. I wanted a little peace and quiet, using the solitude to soak up the atmosphere and to get a feel for this side of the hospital. Although I possess all of the psychic sensitivity of the average brick, even I could tell that there was something unusual about this place. I couldn't quite put my finger on what it was, but it intrigued me nonetheless. It was almost as if the entire place was holding its breath somehow…waiting. I tried to tell myself that it was just my over-active imagination playing tricks on me, but the feeling of being watched by unseen eyes was impossible to shake.

In one of the hallways, a series of cardboard packing boxes had been lined up along either side, placed neatly outside the doorways the led to the residents' rooms. There were two for each room. When I squatted down and gave the contents of one a cursory glance, I realized that the boxes contained the personal effects of the people who had lived there. There was no way I was going to go through the belongings of the men and women who had, until just recently, made this place their home. Each box was a life in miniature, its contents the mementos and keepsakes of somebody who had lived here. They were entitled to their privacy.

I straightened up and walked on, going in and out of the rooms at random. Most of the beds and furniture had been left behind, presumably to be replaced with more modern equivalents at the newer facility.

Cami caught up with me and asked which room I'd like to sleep in over the next few nights. After all, she pointed out, I had the run of the place, and could pick any bedroom in the entire facility.

"Which one has the reputation for being the most haunted?" I asked.

"Room 17," Cami answered without hesitation. "Former staff members have told me that the room had such a bad reputation, they tried not to put patients in there at all, if they could possibly avoid it."

We walked down to the end of the hallway together. Room 17 was at the very end. I turned around and looked back toward the nurses' station, which seemed a very, *very* long way away...and besides, it's not as though there would be anybody staffing it when we slept there anyway. My colleagues and I would be the only people in the entire building. Cami was going to lock us inside; that way, we would know that any bizarre activity would not be down to people coming in from the outside.

A little digging turned up some interesting information on Room 17. Residents of that room had seen a tall, black figure looming over their beds at night. To make things even more alarming, it had possessed a pair of glowing red eyes that never blinked. The shadow figure didn't seem to do much of anything; it simply stood there, staring down at them. That alone would more be more than enough to terrify anybody, and I could see why people didn't like staying in there. When a sweet old lady woke up to find this apparition standing by her bedside, her terrified screams brought the staff running. They ended up relocating her to the opposite end of the hallway, much closer to the nurses' station. While this seemed to mollify her somewhat, the poor woman flatly refused to walk past the halfway point of the hallway ever again.

I'm not one of those people that walks into a supposedly haunted location and 'feels' things, by which I mean, I have little to nothing in the way of psychic sensitivity. On a handful of occasions, I have gotten a vaguely bad feeling about a place — one of my nights at 30 East Drive, aka the 'Black Monk House,' springs to mind — but by and large, I don't tend to feel much in the way of such things.

This was different. I'd already gotten what I can only describe as a weird vibe while walking around the rooms and hallways earlier that day. Now, there was something about Room 17 that set my teeth on edge. Once again, I couldn't say exactly what it was, and the skeptical part of my brain insisted that it was nothing more than me being psychologically pre-disposed to finding the room to be frightening, based on the stories I'd heard about it.

On the face of it, Room 17 didn't look any different than the other rooms I had already explored. It was actually two rooms, connected by a single, short passageway. The room in the back had two beds and a restroom, whereas the room in front only had a single bed. I claimed that room, setting my backpack down on the mattress. My colleague, Jason, and another fellow investigator, went to the room at the back.

Jason took great delight in pointing out that anything that came in from outside in the hallway would get to me first.

After eating dinner, we began setting up equipment for our investigation. Because only a handful of us would be investigating that night, we kept things pretty basic — handheld equipment and a couple of remote cameras.

Night fell, and we got things going. Paranormal investigators tend to work primarily at night, and with very good reason: it isn't true that spirits are more active after dark, but it IS true that the world is a lot quieter at night. There is less traffic on the roads, for example, and fewer people walking the streets…all of which adds up to less potential contamination for our audio recordings. Not to mention the fact that most of us have day jobs…

Most of the first few hours were taken up with EVP sessions, in which we attempted to capture the voices of whichever spirits were present, on digital voice recorders. I was hoping that somebody — *anybody* — would talk to us. Ultimately, we were to be disappointed. Other than our own voices, nothing turned up on the recordings. We remained cheerful about it. That was how things went, most of the time. Deciding to take a break, we headed over to the nurses' station to relax over a cup of tea or coffee.

We called out politely to the spirits of the building, asking them to make their presence known to us in some way, shape, or form. As we stood there, shooting the breeze and chatting amongst ourselves, a loud *boom* sounded from somewhere off to our right.

"What was *that?*" I wanted to know.

"Sounds like it came from down that corridor," Jason said, disappearing off into the darkness. Moments later, his flashlight came on at the far end of the hallway. We watched the beam playing across the walls. Finally, Jason called out that we had better get on over there.

When we got to the end of the hallway, I could see why. On the left were the resident rooms, all of which were dark and empty. On the right were the two heavy wooden doors that separated the ward from the Green Mile. For the past several days, those doors had both stood wide open, as a constant parade of people walked back and forth between them.

Now, in the middle of the night, with hospital completely deserted except for the few of us, one of them had just slammed shut. All by itself.

We spent the next fifteen minutes trying — and ultimately failing — to find a simple explanation for what had happened. Nobody had been anywhere near the doors when the incident had happened. Perhaps it was 'just one of those things,' but if that was the case, then the timing seemed awfully suspicious. (Cami told us several weeks later that once she opened the door back up again, it remained open indefinitely).

Fortunately, the locked-off video camera had captured the door swinging shut. Playing the footage back, it was very apparent that nothing had physically interfered with the door. Was a former resident of the nursing home letting us know that they were still around?

The next few hours were spent trying to connect with some of those people. I have nothing but compassion for those who are in the twilight of their lives, and nothing but respect for those who care for them. There was to be no provocation or yelling. We spoke calmly and respectfully, attempting to coax them out to talk with us, but it just wasn't happening.

"They're still getting used to people like you guys," Cami said, and I wondered whether she meant strangers in general, or paranormal investigators in particular. She had a great point. I tried to look at it from their point of view. For the last few years, any spirits at the nursing home would have gotten used to a very specific routine. They would have seen the same faces coming and going, usually at the same times of day and night. There would have been great comfort and sense of security to be had from that routine...and suddenly, *POOF!* Everything changed. All that was once familiar, was now gone. The building — no, *their home*, I reminded myself — was pretty much empty, save for a few strangers coming and going. No wonder they were shy, and not exactly forthcoming. All things considered, who could blame them?

"I don't think we're going to get anything over here tonight," Jason said, shaking his head. I agreed with him. "So, what do you want to do?"

"Let's head on over to the other side of the hospital," I suggested. "I'd like to look in on Wesley."

During my research for *The Haunting of Asylum 49,* Wesley's story had touched my heart. A long-term resident of the hospital, he had been afflicted with one of the cruelest diseases imaginable: Alzheimer's.

As with many dementia sufferers, Wesley had his good days and his bad days. On his good days, he was a kind and friendly gentleman, smiling and laughing at things he found funny. On the bad, however, it was a very different story. His moods became dark and angry. It was not unknown for him to erupt in sudden, explosive outbursts, during some of which he could become physically violent. Although this made him dangerous to be around, it wasn't his fault. Part of the cruelty of Alzheimer's is its ability to strip away the kinder, gentler parts of the human personality, often when it is least expected.

After his death, Wesley's former room soon gained a reputation for being haunted. Visiting mediums came in, and described a man who matched Wesley's physical and behavioral description almost exactly…so much so, in fact, that a framed pencil sketch of his face is mounted outside the doorway to Wesley's room to this day.

While filming for *Ghost Adventures*, host Zak Bagans spent some time in Wesley's room. From the footage that aired on TV, he treated its incumbent spirit in a very antagonistic way, verbally pushing him to do something.

Wesley quite literally pushed back, shoving an obviously-surprised Bagans back against the wall.

This poor man's story not only touched me on a very personal level, but it also intrigued me in my capacity as a paranormal investigator. Of the many psychic mediums I have spoken to on the subject of life after death, practically all of them agree that when we die, any illnesses, medical conditions, or physical injuries are left behind with the physical body. They should not be carried over into the next life with us.

And yet, those who work, volunteer, and investigate at the old hospital, all seem to agree that Wesley's behavior in death is exactly the same as it was during his lifetime. Visitors to his room can sometimes be rewarded with friendly, almost playful encounters with him, but on the other hand, others have been physically attacked when they enter his space. The first time I spent the night at the old hospital, I left one of my sandwiches for him as an offering of friendship.

Now, whenever I return to the hospital, I like to drop by Wesley's room and pay my respects. If what the mediums claimed was true, and Wesley was still hanging around in the hospital instead of moving on, it didn't sound like a particularly joyful existence to me, and I figured he would appreciate the company.

Cami led our small group along the length of the Green Mile. As we followed the long, sloping hallway down toward the opposite side of the hospital, we kept a close eye out for one of the many shadow figures that are regularly reported. These human-shaped forms are usually seen to be poking their heads out of side rooms, or dashing across from one end of the corridor to the other and back again.

Tonight, the shadows did not move.

We made our way toward the old maternity wing. In the hospital's heyday, this place had echoed with the cries of newborn babies and the laughter of first-time parents. New families were being formed on a daily basis. Now, everything was silent and dark — almost unnaturally so.

The haunted house attraction had ended several months before, but most of the props were still set up. One room that made me particularly wary was home to a beast that was nicknamed the Banshee. Sculpted from latex, this monstrosity had a screaming, demonic-looking face, and grasping claws. Its job was to come flying out of the darkness at high speed, frightening the life out of the unsuspecting visitor who had set it off.

The Banshee was mounted on a sturdy metal frame, one that dominated the doorway of a room just a few feet away from Wesley's. It was launched forward on pneumatic pistons, which were controlled by a very simple electronic circuit.

The last thing we wanted to happen when we were trying to carry out a paranormal investigation, was for one of us to trigger the Banshee, and scare us half to death.

Fortunately, Cami had a solution. She knew everything there was to know about the mechanics of the haunt. "The Banshee is set off by an infra-red beam," she explained, squatting down in the open doorway of its room. "When somebody walks past this doorway, they break the beam, and *voila:* Out it comes. All we have to do is put the beam emitter face-down on the ground. Then there's no possible way that it can be broken."

Cami reached out and carefully unclipped the infra-red beam emitter, and set it down inside the room. The job was done. It was no longer possible for one of us to inadvertently trigger the Banshee.

We sat down on the floor at the end of the hallway. I positioned myself directly opposite the doorway to Wesley's room, then started my digital voice recorder running. If the spirits of the nursing home weren't willing to talk to us, perhaps we would have better luck with him.

Sitting next to me, Jason began using his infra-red camera to record our EVP session. Cami started us off, and then we all pitched in with questions of our own. Requests for knocks, taps, or some other manifestation in the form of physical phenomena, were ignored.

And then...

A loud hiss, like the sound of a giant, angry snake, was accompanied by a violent rattling sound. From just off to my right, the white-clad form of the Banshee emerged from its doorway, where it began shaking as though having some kind of seizure.

"Was that...supposed to happen?" Jason asked, displaying a talent for understatement I had never before known him to possess.

My heart was racing in my chest. It felt almost fit to burst. Part of it was the sudden, unexpected shock, but there was something else. "Cami, you said it was impossible for that thing to go off!"

"It should be!" Cami was confused. She pulled out a flashlight and began inspecting the mechanism, "See, the beam is still unbroken. There's no way it could have set off the Banshee, unless…"

"Unless what?"

"There's a manual trigger," she explained, ducking into the Banshee's room. "A button. But you would have to be inside the room to push it. And there's nobody in here."

Just to be sure, we searched the Banshee's room from top to bottom. As we expected, there wasn't a living soul in there — at least, none that we could see. But *somebody* had to have fired off the Banshee. The manual button had been pushed somehow. The device was very reliable, mechanically speaking, and had never gone off on its own either before that night or since.

Although there was no way for us to be sure, I had the sneaking suspicion that I knew who was responsible. As we were collecting our equipment to go back to the nursing home, I stuck my head around the door of Wesley's room.

"Nice job, my friend," I whispered, with a smile on my face. "You nearly gave me a bloody heart attack!"

The dark and empty room grinned right back at me.

It didn't take long for me to grow to *hate* Room 17.

There was no concrete reason why. I just couldn't sleep

in there. It felt as if I was being watched. Claiming that his foot hurt, one of my room-mates declined to continue the investigation, and went to stay with a friend.

Jason's family soon arrived in town, staying at a hotel, and so he quite understandably went to join them after our nights of investigation.

That left me all on my own in that room. I began to develop a new-found sense of appreciation for the member of the *Ghost Adventures* crew, who had spent a night all alone in the old hospital. He had been woken up in the middle of the night by a loud bang, which turned out to be the sound of one of the doors slamming shut on the nursing home side of the building — exactly what we had experienced, and captured on camera.

It might sound like the easiest thing in the world to crawl into a sleeping back and snooze the night away in a haunted location, but it isn't always that easy. The atmosphere is so thick and heavy in some places that you simply don't want to let down your guard. I've run into a number of places like that during my career as a paranormal investigator, and Room 17 is right at the top of that list.

The skeptical part of my nature can't help but wonder if this is a purely psychological phenomenon. After all, I had indirectly heard all about the room's supposedly terrifying ghostly occupant from those who had worked there. While it was impossible to tell just how much, if any, of those stories were true, it would have been foolish of me to think that my psyche was immune to being affected by them.

I slept with one eye open, as the old saying goes, drifting in and out of sleep and keeping a close watch on the door leading out into the hallway. A number of thumps and bangs came from out there during the hours of darkness, but I attributed them to the structure settling down as the metal beams cooled off.

Eventually, I would drift off to sleep, but it was a restless slumber at best. The sense of unease never quite left me, and by the third night of our stay, I was beginning to seriously regret opening my big mouth and asking permission to stay in this room.

You should have gotten a hotel room instead, you bloody idiot.

To cap things off, the hot water wasn't working, so I had to take ice cold showers in the old patient bathroom. This was great for waking myself up rapidly, but it was a pretty miserable experience nonetheless — I'm embarrassed to admit that as I've gotten older, I've grown to really like my creature comforts.

On our final night, fellow investigator and paramedic Jen took pity on me, and invited me to use the shower in her hotel room. She knew me well enough, having worked with me in the medical field for several years, and could tell that I was not doing well. My spirits were low, and my mood was beginning to be affected. Nor was I the only one.

It started with the little things; an irritated glance here, a few cross words there. It turned out that we had all been arguing amongst ourselves, with no apparent cause for us to do so. We are a tight-knit team of friends, not generally given to squabbling, and yet suddenly we had mothers arguing with daughters, husbands arguing with their wives, and just a general air of unease that tainted the whole investigation.

Now that I was clean (having enjoyed my first hot shower in several days) and had changed into some fresh clothes, I should have started to feel a little bit better…but I didn't. As Jen drove me the short distance back from her hotel to the old hospital, a knot began to twist and grow in the pit of my stomach. I realized, much to my surprise, that I really did *not* want to go back into that building. The nearer we got, the greater my sense of dread became, and while there was no specific reason for it that I could put my finger on, it was a powerful feeling indeed.

Jen parked the car outside the former nursing home. It was still night-time. I sat there, just staring at the darkened windows. Every once in a while, I caught a flash of what seemed to be movement inside. Probably just a trick of the light, I told myself.

We sat there and talked for over an hour. The topics of conversation rambled all over the map. I knew that Jen could read me well enough to know that something was up, and like any good friend, she helped me get through it.

"Jen, I really don't want to go back inside," I admitted a last, more than a little embarrassed.

"I wouldn't either. Something has been off about this whole place since we came to investigate. That's why we're all at one another's throats."

She was absolutely right. Since they had made the nursing home side available, the atmosphere had felt badly 'off' to us. We had all picked up on it, in one way or another, and we were all being affected. For the first time ever, I couldn't wait to leave this place — hands-down my favorite haunted location ever — behind.

Jen didn't give me a hard time about my feeling of

extreme uneasiness. Instead, she sat with me in the car and chatted about nothing in particular until the sun came up. Reluctantly, I got out of the car and made the long walk up to the front doors. When I went inside, all was still and quiet. The atmosphere didn't feel any more welcoming.

The sense of unpleasantness was at its strongest in Room 17. I packed my equipment and bedding up, keeping one eye on the shadows all the time, and went to make my travel arrangements.

If I never saw that the inside of that room again in my life, it would be too soon.

Due to unexpected circumstances, in 2018, the haunt attraction had to be moved from its long-term home across to the nursing home part of the building. Everybody held their breath, wondering just how it would affect the paranormal activity at Asylum 49.

Yet again, I couldn't pass up the opportunity to head out there at Halloween and find out for myself. Clad as a blood-splattered surgeon, I worked the haunt until midnight, relishing the opportunity to help make grown men and women scream in terror. Things took a turn for the surreal when a group of stand-up comedians put on a show in the center of the old nursing home, on the very same night that the haunted house was in full swing. Their jokes were constantly interrupted by a constant parade of shrieking customers running out of the haunt.

Afterward, when the lights were switched out and the last customer had gone home, we locked the doors and settled down to investigate. Surprisingly, this was one of the less active spells I have ever spent there. Although we got some interesting EVPs and had a handful of subjective personal experiences, this wasn't the non-stop stream of paranormal activity that I had grown accustomed to.

It is my belief that, as time passes, the spirits on the nursing home side seem to be growing a little more comfortable with the new status quo. There are a number of shops on-site now, occupying what were once residential rooms. One shop, run by a delightful lady named Julie, is home to a mischievous spirit that likes to throw her wares onto the floor overnight when the store (and building) are locked up tight. This happens too often, and to different pieces of merchandise, for the explanation to be objects simply falling from the shelves.

At the time of writing (June of 2019) construction work

is currently underway on this year's haunt. As the building work ramps up, so does the paranormal activity; this is a cycle that repeats itself every year, a byproduct of the influx of energy that enters the building. Historically speaking, construction and demolition are two well-known triggers for a dormant haunting to flare up once more.

Visitors are no longer permitted to spend the night in the much-feared Room 17; it is currently used for storage purposes only. I can't say that I am disappointed by the fact that I won't be able to sleep there again — that room makes me uncomfortable, as few other places ever have.

The living and the dead have reached a (mostly comfortable) rapprochement at Asylum 49. With one or two negative entities aside, the spirits seem to have adopted a "don't bother us and we won't bother you" attitude toward their flesh-and-blood neighbors. For their part, the owners of the building insist that their resident ghosts be treated with the same respect that any living being should be entitled to.

Nobody wants ripples in the water. Although the spirits still make their presence known — usually in a playful, pranksterish sort of way — the atmosphere inside the old healthcare facility tends to be a friendly and welcoming one.

Long may it remain so.

Acknowledgments

Firstly, to you, the reader: Thank you for spending your hard-earned money and valuable time in order to read this book. It is my sincere hope that you have enjoyed it, and would ask you to *please* consider rating the book on Amazon's website. In the current writing market, books tend to live and die by their reviews and ratings, particularly on Amazon. Your help would therefore be greatly appreciated.

Some other thanks are due to the people without whom this book would not have been possible, beginning with those who allowed me to share their stories.

Judy Leesee
Richelle Glands
Trish Quinn
Jill Reazor
Gemma Lee Drury
Angela Rippy-Burgett
Daniel Rolfe
Kimm & Cami Andersen, Dusty Kingston, and the Asylum 49 family
Richard Rolfe

Emma Hansen

Glynis Allen

MJ Dickson, for writing the introduction

Laura, for all of her support.

My para-friends and family across Britain, the U.S. and Canada. I wish there were room to thank you all personally here for all that you do.

If you feel so inclined, please visit me over at my web page, www.richardestep.net. I love to hear from readers, so drop by and say hi!

Much love,
Richard

Printed in Great Britain
by Amazon